PORTFOLIO
FUNDING YOUR START-UP

DR DHRUV NATH is a professor at the Management Development Institute, Gurgaon. He is also an active angel investor and a director with Lead Angels. He has invested in over ten start-ups and has mentored several others. He was earlier a senior vice president with NIIT Ltd.

Dr Nath has been a consultant to the top management of several organizations such as Glaxo, Gillette, Nestle, Indian Oil Corporation, Thermax and Bajaj Auto, as well as to the prime minister of Namibia and the chief minister of Delhi.

He has written three books, published by McGraw-Hill Education. He has a BTech in electrical engineering and a PhD in computer science, both from IIT Delhi.

He can be reached at dhruvn55@gmail.com

SUSHANTO MITRA has been associated with the early-stage start-up ecosystem in India for more than fifteen years, with prior experience in consulting and financial services. He founded Lead Angels with a team of three, all from IIT Bombay. Today Mitra has taken the network to more than 130 members and a full-time team of twelve people. The company is now a full-stack financial services provider for start-ups, covering advisory and professional services. He was earlier the founding CEO of Society for Innovation and Entrepreneurship (SINE), IIT Bombay, and the director of Hyderabad Angels. He frequently speaks at industry events and writes for business journals.

He can be reached at sushanto@leadangels.in

FUNDING YOUR START-UP
and Other Nightmares

DHRUV NATH
SUSHANTO MITRA

Foreword by Sanjeev Bikhchandani

PORTFOLIO
PENGUIN

An imprint of Penguin Random House

PORTFOLIO

USA | Canada | UK | Ireland | Australia
New Zealand | India | South Africa | China

Portfolio is part of the Penguin Random House group of companies
whose addresses can be found at global.penguinrandomhouse.com

Published by Penguin Random House India Pvt. Ltd.
4th Floor, Capital Tower 1, MG Road,
Gurugram 122 002, Haryana, India

First published in Portfolio by Penguin Random House India 2020

ISBN 9780143450382

Typeset in Adobe Garamond Pro by Manipal Technologies Limited, Manipal
Printed at Replika Press Pvt. Ltd, India

www.penguin.co.in

Contents

Contents

Foreword

The Indian start-up scene has seen an explosion in recent years—and I don't need to tell you that. Of course, it remains to be seen how this will be impacted by COVID-19. However, I believe that after some weeding out of fragile start-ups, the underlying trend of a boom in start-ups will resume—albeit with a little bit more trepidation and caution, and more measured risk-taking.

Of course, you've heard the big names—Flipkart, MakeMyTrip, Ola Cabs, Paytm and our very own Naukri.com. Venture capital firms such as Sequoia Capital, Lightspeed, SoftBank, SAIF Partners, Matrix Partners and others have put their money in Indian start-ups and hopefully will continue to do so.

There are perhaps more than 20,000 registered start-ups in India, and the number of unregistered ones is likely to be several times more. Everyone is searching for their El Dorado—what is popularly known as a unicorn, or a valuation of a billion dollars. In this environment, I'm not surprised that more and more youngsters—and some oldies as well—have jumped on to the start-up bandwagon. And since you've picked up this book and are actually reading it, I assume you are one of them.

Great. Welcome to the club. I respect your decision. And now the question is: What should you do? Well, in the twenty-plus years we have spent in starting and growing our own companies Naukri.com, 99acres.com and Jeevansaathi.com, and through our own experience of investing in more than two dozen start-ups, we have learnt a lot. We have experimented with business models, tried out multiple options and backtracked when required. At times we have even gone into hibernation to think!

Fortunately, I have had many opportunities to pass on some of this learning to young start-ups. I have been mentoring and advising some of them, and I enjoy doing that.

The problem, of course, is that one cannot possibly meet all the thousands and thousands of founders out there. And that is why I am delighted that Dhruv and Sushanto have written a book on the subject. That, too, on the extremely important subject of fundraising. I have known both of them for several decades now. Sushanto has been involved in the start-up scene for more than twenty years, culminating in the launch of Lead Angels six years ago. We have had several occasions to discuss the start-up scene in India, and I must say he is extremely knowledgeable and passionate about the subject. Dhruv and I have been on panel discussions together, and I was impressed with his clarity of thought, as well as his ability to explain complex subjects in a simple manner. Interestingly, the ideas of both Dhruv and Sushanto are more or less similar to mine, so much of the advice they share in this book is perhaps advice I, too, would have given you. And, therefore, I genuinely believe that they are the right people to write such a book and advise founders.

Ultimately, you need to learn from others, and the authors have described several start-ups in this book—all in the form of interesting stories. I'm particularly delighted that they have taken up a wide range of start-ups. On the one hand, they have taken expert advice from some of the highly successful founders in the start-up world, such as Deep Kalra of MakeMyTrip, Yashish Dahiya of PolicyBazaar,

Dinesh Agarwal of IndiaMART, Pradeep Gupta of CyberMedia, Nakul Kumar of Cashify and Sairee Chahal of SHEROES. But they have also spoken about much smaller start-ups—those that have started recently and are rarely spoken about. And finally, and perhaps most importantly, they have discussed some failures as well. Now that's really great, because no one talks about the failures—and, therefore, potential entrepreneurs can never learn from the mistakes they have made.

I like the fact that Dhruv and Sushanto have tried to create a framework for potential start-ups, which they call 'PERSISTENT'. Running a company is a complex business, and raising funds equally so. You need guidelines that you can refer to from time to time, and that's what the PERSISTENT framework provides. Mind you, it's not a formula—it cannot be—but it's a very good set of guidelines. And that's exactly what the authors have said in this book—the PERSISTENT framework is a set of guidelines that you should keep referring to throughout your journey.

So let's get down to some specifics. I believe the most important thing in determining the success of your start-up is to identify the right opportunity. I would say it's 60 per cent of the recipe for success—where you have identified an unsolved problem and have a solution for it, and where the customer comes to you rather than you chasing the customer. This is the starting point for the PERSISTENT framework in the book. Namely: 'Are you solving a problem, and will people pay for it? How are you doing it better than competition? And what's your ENTRY BARRIER?'

Now for the subject of funding. Always remember, the customer's money is much better than the investor's money—as long as it is coming in regularly, and is higher than your costs. Because you then have a viable business. This is especially important in the post COVID-19 world. And if you are getting the customer's money, you will almost certainly get the investor's money. This has been explained in this book as part of the EARNINGS MODEL, once again within the PERSISTENT framework.

Very importantly, don't build a business with the objective of selling it in the next few years. Building a business is a lifetime's commitment. And please don't focus on becoming a unicorn. Focus on your customers—which will ultimately benefit your investors. If you get obsessed with valuations, you will lose focus and ultimately your customers. Valuation should not be an aim. Building a solid business should be your aim. Build a solid business, and valuations will follow. Once again, the authors have stressed on this several times in the book, and specifically in the chapter on valuations.

Once you've got the money, what do you do with it? Well, once again, I agree with what the authors have stressed on in this book. Namely, treat the investor's money as sacred. The fact that you've got the money doesn't mean the commitment ends—it has just begun. Do you know what to do with the investor's money? Will you spend it smartly? Great companies are capital-efficient. And for this you need to build good habits. Right in the beginning of your venture, don't take too much money, and don't take it too early. Companies that either get too much money or get it too easily tend to use it suboptimally. You can spot the symptoms—fancy offices, fancy salaries, fancy off-sites. Learn to be frugal—because then you build a more sustainable business. And a good way to be frugal is to be slightly scarce with the cash you have. You don't value money if it is too freely available.

In the final analysis, your reputation is your only asset. If your company succeeds, and you have given your investors a good exit, you have a better chance of getting funding when you plan to start a new venture. And even if your company fails, the investor should feel that you as the entrepreneur were okay, and should be willing to invest in you again. Once again, in this book, the authors have spoken about companies that failed, but where the entrepreneur was great—and therefore would certainly attract investors once again.

And, finally, I believe the 'PERSISTENT' framework that the authors have come up with is highly appropriate. You cannot create a great company in two or three years. A great company takes a decade or more to build. Your mantra has to be patience and persistence. Remember, *company khoon paseene se banti hai* (a company is built with your sweat and hard work).

To summarize, any entrepreneur will find this book a great guide for successfully creating and growing a start-up. I would strongly recommend that you read it, and keep referring to it from time to time. As I have said earlier, the advice you'll get from my friends Dhruv and Sushanto is very similar to what you will get from me. So have fun reading it, and I'm sure you'll benefit from it.

—Sanjeev Bikhchandani
Founder and vice chairman, Naukri.com

Section I

The Fascinating World of Start-Up Funding

1

Introduction

So you want to create a start-up? Or have already created one?

How did we guess? Simple. You wouldn't be reading this book otherwise!

Either way, you are probably stuck for funds, aren't you?

Aha! Welcome, my friend! Welcome to the gang of 'founders-who-are-desperate-for-funds-but-are-unable-to-raise-them-and-are-therefore-frustrated-as-hell'. This is where most start-ups get stuck. Many are not able to raise any funding at all. Others raise the first round from angel investors but cannot raise subsequent rounds from venture capital funds. Only a few are able to raise multiple rounds and are, therefore, able to grow rapidly and continuously. So welcome to this book on raising funds for your start-up.

Now there are several books available on the subject of start-ups, but there don't seem to be too many on the specific subject of funding—especially in the Indian context. In other words, a book that talks about what investors look for at various stages of a start-up and, therefore, what the start-up needs to do to catch their interest. And, by the way, that is why we have written this book—to help start-up founders raise funding! So keep reading, and hopefully we'll be able to help you. Just sit back, pick up a cup of coffee—or beer, if you prefer—and let's go . . .

Incidentally, as you may have guessed, we are focusing largely on early-stage funding—what we call the angel round and series A (more about these terms later). After all, if you happen to be Bhavish Aggarwal of Ola Cabs, and want to raise a couple of billion dollars, you probably have enough advisers to help you anyway. You will probably not pick up this book. But if you are a recent start-up and need help, well, this book is for you.

And now a bit of background. When we decided to write this book, we realized that it would have to be stories. About start-ups. Because the best way to increase your chances of success is to learn from other start-ups, since many of them would have faced similar situations and problems. And so we decided on stories. Definitely not theory. Too, too boring. And we're sure you, as the reader, would agree.

Having settled the question of stories, the next question was: Which start-ups do we write about? Most books tend to talk about the major international success stories—Google, Amazon, Facebook, Uber, WhatsApp, and the like. Sure, you can learn from these guys. And you should. But isn't it far more important to learn from companies in the Indian context? After all, you are creating a start-up in India, aren't you? As you are undoubtedly aware, the Indian environment is very, very different from what exists in the West. For instance, infrastructure is certainly not at the same level—which is a constraint, but also an opportunity. It's a far more price-conscious market than many others. If you are looking at a B2B start-up, you need to plan for the fact that many payments in India get delayed. To summarize, therefore, while you should learn from start-ups in the United States, it's much more critical to learn from start-ups in India. (Of course, if you are planning to start something in the Belgian Congo or in Zimbabwe, please ignore our advice and learn from start-ups there.)

So that's clear—you need to learn from Indian start-ups. Now the next question. You have a huge range of such start-ups. You have the big guns—the market leaders, the highly successful ones. Those who are household names today. Names such as Naukri.com, MakeMyTrip, PolicyBazaar, Flipkart and Oyo Rooms, to name a few. Names that are respected, and whose founders are spoken about in hushed tones over the inevitable pegs of Black Label. Wouldn't you like to learn from them? Sure you would.

And then we have the smaller guys. Start-ups that began recently, are still relatively small and have struggled their way through. Start-ups that are facing the same problems today that you are facing. Start-ups that you can really identify with—rather like the boy or girl next door whom you can talk to. Wouldn't you like to learn from them as well? Sure, once again.

So we have an interesting situation, where any budding start-up would like to learn from today's highly successful unicorns and their eminent founders, but at the same time, learn from peers that are struggling to stay afloat. And, therefore, we have a question for you: Whom would you rather learn from?

Tough choice, isn't it? But guess what? You don't need to make a choice. Because we've got both in this book. We've got lots of stories about start-ups that are still start-ups—those that you can sit with over a cup of coffee at your friendly neighbourhood café. Essentially, your peers. And we also have those about successful founders in the business—Sanjeev Bikhchandani of Naukri.com, Deep Kalra of MakeMyTrip, Yashish Dahiya of PolicyBazaar, Dinesh Agarwal of IndiaMART, Nakul Kumar of Cashify and Sairee Chahal of SHEROES. And to top it all, we've got a couple of the best-known investors in the business, namely Pradeep Gupta, the co-founder of Indian Angel Network, and Rajul Garg, the founder of Leo Capital. They have all been happy to share their advice—which we've promptly included in this book. So you are in the happy position of learning from both the big guns and the smaller guys.

Now for a very, very important issue: You can get lots of material about start-ups that succeeded. Those who raised angel funding, or even multiple rounds of funding. But what about those that failed to do so? Shouldn't you be learning from them as well? To take an analogy from the film industry, if you want to be an actor, it is good to learn from Shah Rukh Khan. But isn't it even more important to learn from those who came from their villages to try their luck in Bollywood, failed and went back to their fields?

Agreed? So how often have you read about start-ups that could not raise funds and, therefore, had to shut down? Never? We certainly haven't. Simply because these things are kept under wraps. Their founders do not talk about them, except to their close friends— usually over liberal amounts of alcohol. They are not written about. And, therefore, no one really knows what went wrong and why they were unable to get money.

That, ladies and gentlemen, is where this book gets really exciting (at least to us, the authors). Both of us have spent several years with young start-ups, investing in them as well as mentoring a few hundreds. There have been some successes but there have also been a fair share of failures. And we decided, in our wisdom, to write about both the success stories as well as the failures we have seen. Failures that have not been written about, and where the learning is not available to other budding start-ups. Of course, in the case of failures, we have sometimes hidden the names of both the start-ups and their founders. And we're sure you will appreciate this.

Finally, you would agree that reading too many stories can get very confusing. After all, each start-up is doing something different. Two start-ups may do the same thing, but one fails and the other succeeds. So what do you learn from them? And what do you do, other than looking and feeling utterly confused?

Dear reader, we understand completely. But remember, we have spent time with lots of start-ups over the past several years. We have seen successes and also failures. And based on this experience, we have created a framework called PERSISTENT, as follows:

- P: Problem. Are you solving a problem? Will people pay?
- E: Earnings model
- R: Risks and how you will mitigate them
- S: Size of the market
- I: Innovation
- S: Scalability
- T: Team, starting with the founders
- E: Entry barriers
- N: Niche. Where the entire market is crowded, identify a large niche
- T: Traction

Interestingly, successful start-ups tend to follow this PERSISTENT model, whereas failures usually miss out on one or more parameters, such as Size of the market, Team or Risks. Therefore, it is useful to evaluate your start-up within this framework.

Now, clearly, investors want to invest in successful start-ups as well. And, therefore, they follow more or less the same approach when evaluating start-ups, although the terms they use may be different. Consequently, all the start-ups in this book have been evaluated using the PERSISTENT approach. Hopefully, by the end of the book, you will be able to use this approach to evaluate your own start-up—and therefore figure out what you need to do to increase the chances of success, as well as the likelihood of getting funding.

And this is where we come to the burning question of today. What do you do in today's post-coronavirus world? Or in a world that has been impacted by some other unexpected crisis, such as the financial crisis of 2008, where money has become scarce, and therefore investors have become more choosy than before? Well, there are many things you need to do, and we'll talk about them as we go through this book. But for a start, remember, if the investor has become more choosy, it means he will only invest in those start-ups that have a greater chance of succeeding. And that means . . .

Those start-ups that follow the PERSISTENT approach. So in today's tough times, there is even more reason to make your start-up PERSISTENT.

One final comment. Is PERSISTENT a foolproof formula? Don't be silly. There is no such thing. It is a set of guidelines that you can follow. It will hopefully increase your chances of succeeding and getting funding. But as you know, in life and in business, there is never any magic formula for success!

So have lots of fun starting and running your start-up. Learn from the successes and failures that we will share with you right here in this book.

And from both of us authors, all the very best to you. May your story be told in the next edition of this book!

2

The Basics of Funding

All set? Okay, let's look at some of the headlines that have been hitting the media over the past couple of years:

'Tiger Global invests $200 million in BYJU's; valuation jumps to $8 billion'[*]
'Walmart completes deal to buy Flipkart for $16 billion'[†]
'India Startup Oyo Raises $1.5 Billion at $10 Billion Valuation'[‡]

_____

[*] Nandita Mathur and Salman SH, 'Tiger Global invests $200 million in BYJU's; valuation jumps to $8 billion', Livemint, 10 January 2020, https://www.livemint.com/companies/start-ups/tiger-global-invests-200-million-in-byju-s-11578570528442.html

[†] Anirban Sen, 'Walmart completes deal to buy Flipkart for $16 billion', Livemint, 18 August 2018, https://www.livemint.com/Companies/qOBduC3OBVpKTv9CpCYayH/Walmart-completes-16billion-buyout-of-Flipkart.html

[‡] Saritha Rai, 'India Startup Oyo Raises $1.5 Billion at $10 Billion Valuation', Bloomberg, 7 October 2019, https://www.bloomberg.com/news/articles/2019-10-07/india-startup-oyo-raises-1-5-billion-at-10-billion-valuation

'Warren Buffett's Berkshire Hathaway closes $300-million investment in Paytm'*

'Chinese investors are suddenly in love with Indian startups'†

Sounds mouth-watering, doesn't it? Now here are some more:

'India emerges 3rd largest ecosystems for successful startups'‡

'Indian startups raised about $14.5 Bn equity funding in 2019'§

Yes sir, this is boom time in India's start-up world. And everyone seems to be getting massive rounds of funding. From angel investors, from VCs, from the US, China, Japan and, of course, India. Everyone is getting funding. *And, therefore, so can you.*

However, you must remember that the companies we have just spoken about raised this kind of funding after years and years of growth. And your own start-up is perhaps still in its early stages. You may get there, but you need to start small. So let's take it one step at a time, and examine how you will start raising money. Beginning with the first step—namely the 'family and friends' round.

---

* Alnoor Peermohamed, 'Warren Buffett's Berkshire Hathaway closes $300-million investment in Paytm', Business Standard, 28 September 2018, https://www.business-standard.com/article/companies/warren-buffett-s-berkshire-hathaway-closes-300-million-investment-in-paytm-118092700876_1.html

† T.E. Narasimhan, 'Chinese investors are suddenly in love with Indian startups', Rediff.com, 2 January 2020, https://www.rediff.com/business/report/tech-chinese-investors-are-in-love-with-indian-startups/20200102.htm

‡ PTI, 'India emerges 3rd largest ecosystems for successful startups', *The Economic Times*, 17 October 2019, https://economictimes.indiatimes.com/small-biz/startups/newsbuzz/india-emerges-3rd-largest-ecosystems-for-successful-startups/articleshow/71636451.cms?from=mdr

§ Jitendra Singh, 'Indian startups raised about $14.5 Bn equity funding in 2019', Entrackr, 27 December 2019, https://entrackr.com/2019/12/startups-raised-about-14-5-bn-equity-funding-in-2019/

The 'Family and Friends' Round

When you create a start-up, you obviously need money. For hiring people, for marketing your product or service, for developing and hosting your website, for operations such as managing inventory and deliveries, for the call centre that will handle calls to and from customers, and for just about anything else that your business requires. And the first place you'll check for money is your own savings. Hopefully, you still have some left after all the mandatory partying that life requires. Having done that, you'll probably go to your father, or your *chacha* or *mama*, and beg for money (begging is perhaps an exaggeration, but you get the idea). If you've maintained decent relations with your chacha or mama, there is a reasonable chance that you'll get something out of them. Even if the reason is as simple as, '*Chal beti* (or *beta*), *zindagi mein kuchh toh kaam kar le* (At least get something done in life).' And then, of course, there are your friends—the ones who are not already neck-deep in debt because of their own start-ups. So that's the first round of funding— the 'family and friends' round.

Now there are a couple of important issues that you must note here. First of all, all these people know you—or, at least, they think they do. You are not an unknown outsider who cannot be trusted (we will ignore the distinct possibility that you are a known person and therefore cannot be trusted). And, therefore, they might be willing to take a risk with you. *Something that an external investor will not do.* Maybe, just maybe, they also see some promise in you. Yes, they will probably look at your business, but they may not want to see the balance sheet of your company. In fact, they might even be willing to fund your idea even before it has taken off, because they know you. On the flip side, however, the amount they put in is likely to be small. To summarize, at this early stage you may be able to raise small amounts from your friends and family, without too many questions being asked.

And then, of course, you start your venture—and soon discover that you need far more funding. By now, of course, your chacha or mama say no, and, most likely, so do your friends. But you do need the money, so where do you go?

To angel investors, of course!

Angel Investors

Angel investors are the first external investors in your business. *Those who do not know you.* Why are they willing to invest in your business? Very simply because they want to make money. They have tried fixed deposits and debt funds, and have learnt that they don't make more than 7 per cent or so—and, of course, they pay tax on this interest. Some of them have tried out the stock market and made money, but they have realized that stock markets can at best give you around 15 per cent returns over the long term. That's it. Real estate is a good option, but the amounts involved are very large and the investments are illiquid. And anyway, real estate seems to be stagnating, at least in the foreseeable future . . .

And therefore, investors are constantly on the lookout for new avenues of investment. Something that can potentially get them much higher returns than these traditional investment options. Where they can park a small part of their investments, even if the risks are substantially higher. And what better place for this than start-ups?

Look at it this way. What are our unicorns such as Flipkart, Oyo Rooms and Ola Cabs valued at? Over a billion dollars each, isn't it? And in some cases, several billion dollars—Flipkart, for instance, was valued at $21 billion when Walmart bought it. Now, can you buy shares in any of these companies at this valuation? Unless you are a direct descendant of some royal family and have inherited pots of gold, certainly not. But—and this is a very important but—could you have bought shares in these companies when they were toddlers and just about starting off? Aha! Sure you could have. And that, ladies and gentlemen, is the concept of the angel investor. QED.

Angel investors—sometimes simply called angels—are people who are either rich or at least comfortably off, and are looking at investing in companies at an early stage. In the hope that they will become the next Flipkart or Naukri.com. And since they have invested at an early stage, they own a large chunk of the company's shares, whose value could increase dramatically when these companies grow ever so rapidly. So the word 'angel' is probably a bit of a misnomer—they are very, very keen to make money. But they are also willing to take a risk. They are, therefore, willing to help you out with funding when your business has not really stabilized and no one else is willing to fund you. And that is how they came to be called 'angel' investors. After all, angels are those who help you when you're in trouble, isn't it?

However, to get back to earth, we know that all start-ups will not become unicorns. Many will simply die out. Some will plod along. But there will be those few success stories that will either become unicorns, or will be bought out by those that do. And that is what angels hope for. To invest in several companies in the hope that at least one of them grows rapidly and becomes a unicorn. Or is bought out by someone, who in turn is bought out by someone . . . till one of these 'someones' becomes a unicorn. The other start-up investments may be worthless, but that doesn't matter—the angel is looking for those one or two start-ups that will make so much money for him that they take care of the losses of all the others put together. Now can you see the lure of angel-investing?

Most angels operate in groups, rather like a pack of wolves—although, hopefully, the similarity ends there. We call these groups 'angel networks'. Each of these networks have several angels as members, and organize regular meetings—typically monthly or quarterly ones. If you are looking for funding, you would need to apply to one or more of these networks. Subsequently, the network goes through a process of shortlisting, based on which a few of the start-ups are selected. These shortlisted start-ups are then asked to come to the next angel meeting and make a presentation—which we also called a 'pitch session'. Here, the angels decide which start-ups they would like to study further for possible investments. This process is described in detail in Chapter 16 of this book.

For the moment, however, we'd just like to emphasize a couple of points. First, while angels operate in groups, their investment decisions are taken individually. The network might help its members in evaluating businesses and doing the necessary due diligence, but investing in each start-up is solely the decision of the individual angel. Secondly, the kind of money raised at this stage is typically between Rs 50 lakh and Rs 2 crore, with each angel putting in anything from Rs 5 lakh upwards. Indian Angel Network, Lead Angels Network and Mumbai Angels are a few of the well-known angel networks in operation when we were writing this book. By the way, many cities have their own networks, such as Chennai Angels, Hyderabad Angels, Jaipur Angels, Chandigarh Angels, etc. Interestingly, given the small amounts that each angel needs to invest, namely Rs 5 lakh, many of these angels are what we call 'aam aadmi angels'—those who are not super rich but still invest in start-ups. And then, of course, we have the real heavyweights—the super angels, such as the Infosys founders, Ratan Tata, Azim Premji, Sachin and Binny Bansal and Vijay Shekhar Sharma. Unlike aam aadmi angels, these super angels do not need networks. Once they decide on a start-up, they often decide to invest the entire amount in the start-up themselves.

Now let's assume you have raised your angel round. And hopefully you grow. And grow. And at some stage you need more money for more growth. Probably more money and at a higher valuation. Perhaps a million dollars, or the equivalent in rupees. Now that is typically beyond the reach of most angels. But you still need the money, so who do you go to?

Venture capitalists, of course!

Venture Capitalists

As you are aware, a venture capitalist, or a VC, manages a fund that takes in investments from either HNIs—high networth individuals—or even organizations. These funds then invest the money in start-ups, but usually at a later stage compared to angels. Now what we are about to say is extremely important, so please pay attention. No drowsing or nodding off.

Angels invest their own money, whereas VCs typically invest other people's money.

How does that make a difference? Simple. If you are an angel investor and you happen to like a great but risky idea, you might be willing to put in a bit of your money. But if you are a VC, would you take the same level of risk with someone else's money? Clearly not (of course, if you do, you can never become a VC. Or, more likely, you will not remain a VC!). Which is one of the reasons why angels make early-stage investments and VCs make later-stage investments. Because at an early stage, the business is not proven and, therefore, risky. At a later stage, the business has stabilized, at least to some extent, the dud companies have been weeded out and, hopefully, investments carry lower risks. And that, ladies and gentlemen, is why VCs invest at a later stage, when a start-up has proved itself.

The other difference is that VCs invest larger amounts, which ties in very well with the fact that at later stages, start-ups do need much more funding. Typically around Rs 5–7 crore and above. Or if you find dollars more exciting, a million dollars and above. The flip side, of course, is, with the business having stabilized to some extent, valuations are also higher.

Don't get us wrong. Nowhere are we saying that VC investments are guaranteed to succeed. Of course not. But the business is more proven and, therefore, the risks are lower. And so, today we have lots of VCs around, looking for those juicy investments. Sequoia Capital, SAIF Partners, Bessemer Venture Partners, Tiger Global Management, SoftBank and Lightspeed Venture Partners are just some of them. And then there are the so-called micro VCs such as Blume Ventures, India Quotient and YourNest Venture Capital. These VCs typically get in at earlier stages and invest amounts that are somewhere between angels and conventional VCs.

And now for some yummy terms. Every industry has its own fancy terms, which people in that industry love to bandy around.

So the computer guys talk about blockchain, Hadoop, augmented reality and so on. The bankers talk about bond yields, spreads, NIMs (net interest margins), etc. The auto industry brags about electric vehicles, hybrids and Bharat Stage VI. So what about our VC industry? Shouldn't it have its own unique terms that VCs can throw around at parties? Sure they do. And their terms are Series A, Series B, Series C . . . all through the letters of the alphabet. And sometimes, just to confuse you, there is also a Pre-Series A . . .

Sounds like fun? You bet it is. These are simply stages of investment. So a Series A investment typically raises $1–3 million, a Series B raises $3–5 million, a Series C raises $5–10 million, and so on. You get the idea, don't you? Series A is typically the first investment by a VC fund, Series B is the next one, and so on. And each stage gets a larger quantum of funding than the previous one. Of course, you must remember that these are only ballpark figures. So you could have a Series A investment that raises less than $1 million, or more than $3 million. There is no law against it. Just remember that Series A precedes Series B, which, in turn, precedes Series C, and so on. And that also tells you what a Pre-Series A investment is. Something that is significantly less than a million dollars, but comes only after an angel round.

Dear reader, do you realize how important this section is? Because you are now armed with just the right set of terms with which to impress people at your next party. And if you drop these terms somewhat nonchalantly, as though you deal with such boring things every day, we can assure you that the effect on your listeners will be quite powerful.

IPO

If you have just about launched your start-up, you don't need to worry about IPOs, or initial public offerings—simply because it's likely to be very, very far into the future. If at all. Essentially, you have to worry about it when getting your shares listed on the stock exchange, through an IPO. Now why would you raise an IPO? Well, there are many reasons. First of all, it gives all the investors—including the employees who may have got ESOPs (Employee Stock Option Plans)—an easy exit through the stock market. Valuations become clearly defined. And, of course, the special powers of the VC that the shareholder agreement provides (see Chapter 20) are gone. By the way, most start-ups never reach this stage. Biggies such as Ola Cabs, Paytm, Flipkart and Oyo Rooms never had an IPO. They simply kept raising larger and larger rounds of funding from VCs. On the other hand, you have Info Edge (the owners of Naukri.com) and IndiaMART, which have both floated IPOs.

Why Raise External Funding?

Good question. The first reason is obvious and we've mentioned it earlier—friends and family can only help up to a point, and when you need larger amounts of money to scale up rapidly, you need to go to outsiders. That much is clear.

But that's not the only reason. Remember investors—whether angels or VCs—are typically highly experienced. And therefore they can add tremendous value to your start-up through mentorship. Because they now own part of your company and are therefore interested in seeing it grow and succeed. Also, they bring solid contacts, which your start-up can use. For instance, if you have a B2B start-up, just imagine the senior-level contacts—and therefore potential clients—your investors could get you. And then, of course, the company gets credibility—so if a biggie such as Sequoia Capital or SoftBank were to invest in you, well, your customers would start respecting you, wouldn't they? To summarize, money, experience, contacts and credibility are all key reasons to look at investors for funding.

But hang on. Does every start-up need funding? Let's just step back for a moment. Look at successful businesses around you. Look at that highly popular photo studio in your neighbourhood. Is that a business? Yes. Is that a successful business? Of course it is. Did they raise any rounds of funding? Most likely not—except perhaps from their family. And what about the highly rated nursing home just two streets away? Once again, highly successful, but which probably never raised any funding, except maybe a bank loan. In fact, you will see successful businesses all around you that are doing great work and perhaps minting money—just look at the Jaguars parked outside their homes. But most of them would never have raised external funding. In fact, we are fairly certain that only a small percentage of ventures actually take funding from outside.

So why has funding become so essential? The answer is media, parties and peers! 'I just raised a Series A round,' brags a founder at a get-together with friends. Of course, he forgets to mention that his venture is loss-making and is likely to remain so for a long, long time. But that's irrelevant. He's raised a Series A round—that's what matters. And the poor guy listening to him, who is actually running a profitable business without needing funding, feels left out. 'Maybe I'm wrong. Maybe I do need money,' he thinks. Or take the media. Every channel and its uncle blares out, 'XYZ company raises a Series B round.' Or, 'PQR valued at over 100 million dollars.' And the poor chap watching feels left out once again. You see? The environment is abuzz with valuations—Series A, B, C, bridge rounds, VCs and the like. And whether you like it or not, peer pressure forces you to act. '*Tune abhi tak* Series A *raise nahin kara? Koi problem hai kya?* (You mean you haven't raised a Series A yet? Is there a problem?)' And so on.

Does that mean you do not require funding? Of course not! If you are building a solid product, you would most likely need money to build it. If you are in a business where rapid growth is the only way to stay ahead of competition, yes, you would definitely need funding—perhaps lots of it. If you are trying to build a consumer brand, you have no choice—you must raise money. But please remember, funding is not something you raise because it is fashionable. It is not something you do when your girlfriend (or boyfriend) starts drifting towards Mr (or Ms) Series B. It is something to be raised if and when you need it. Remember, funding is not an end in itself—funding is a means to an end, and that end is to run a successful, profitable business. Yes, if you do need it, there is no option and you must raise it.

Also, even if you do need to raise money, funding and valuations should not be your focus. Focus on building your business. If you can do that, the funding will come. Don't chase funding. Build a successful business, and let funding chase you.

The Impact of the Coronavirus—or Any Other Crisis

Dear founder, that's a huge question. And at least part of the answer is obvious: Businesses have slowed down, even if temporarily. People have lost money. Most of them are not willing to take risks at the moment and are happy to park their money in a fixed deposit with their friendly neighbourhood bank. So what happens to angels? They are also people, aren't they? Quite naturally, they have also become risk-averse. That doesn't mean they will not invest, but they will perhaps be far more choosy. And that brings us back to our favourite theme—ensure that your start-up is PERSISTENT, and you stand a better chance of getting angel funds.

By the way, this is true for any crisis, and not just COVID-19. When funds are in short supply, PERSISTENT is the way to go.

But what about VCs? Well, that's a slightly different story. Remember that angels have a choice—they can park their money in bank fixed deposits. But the VC cannot. VCs have raised funds for a limited period, and they need to give returns to their investors. And so they will go ahead and invest. What's the message for you, dear founder? Well, if your start-up is at a later stage and you need VC money, you will probably find it a bit easier. But, of course, you still need to be PERSISTENT.

And with that, we come to the end of this chapter. We have looked at different kinds of investors, and we have also looked at different stages of investment. We've seen why you need to raise funding. And why you don't. And now, assuming you do, wouldn't you like to look at the real thing? Wouldn't you like to meet start-ups that have actually gone through these stages? Including those that managed to raise funding? And even more important, those that could not and fell by the wayside? Wouldn't you like to understand the PERSISTENT approach?

We're sure you would. And for that, there is one simple thing you need to do.

Just turn the page.

Section II

Early-Stage Funding

Those Who Made It and Those Who Couldn't

3

The Cute Story of MyCuteOffice*

Abhishek Barari was having a cup of coffee with a few friends in a neighbourhood café in Mumbai. It was 2014, and his friends were running start-ups of their own. And they were all complaining about rents in the city.

'It's impossible to get a place to work in,' one of them said. 'I only want a one-room office, but that's just not available in the area that I want! Those that are available are either too far away or too expensive. And I've got to furnish it, maintain it, organize tea and coffee for my guys—it's just too much. I want to run my business, not be an office administrator!' one of them said, and glared at his coffee. (Note for the reader: This was during the time that co-working spaces had not become popular and were rarely available.)

The conversation turned to the Indian cricket team's tour of Australia, but somewhere at the back of Abhishek's mind, the problem stayed. Even when his childhood hero M.S. Dhoni was being discussed, he had a thoughtful look on his face, and wasn't

---

* Taken from the authors' personal interviews with Abhishek Barari between 2015 and 2020.

really listening. While on his way home, the thought persisted and he kept wondering what to do about it.

That night, Abhishek was unable to sleep peacefully. He dreamt that he was on his knees in front of three landlords, all of whom refused to give him their miserable, stupid office space, for as ridiculous a reason as rent. He told them repeatedly that his business would grow rapidly and he would soon be able to increase the rent he was paying, but the idiots simply refused to listen. He woke up feeling dejected, and decided to go and meet another friend who ran his own business nearby.

While sitting with him, Abhishek looked around casually and noticed an empty room in the office.

'Don't you need this space?' he asked.

'Not for the next few years,' his friend replied.

'And you own this office, don't you?' Abhishek asked, but he wasn't really listening. Suddenly he had found the answer to Mumbai's office-space problem. Why not rent out partial office spaces? If someone had an office where a room, or even part of a room, was free, why not rent it out to someone who wanted only one room, or maybe just a couple of desks?

And Abhishek jumped up! Why couldn't he, Abhishek Barari, be the person who brought the landlord and the tenant together?

Landlords would love to get the additional rent for their vacant space, and tenants would be equally delighted to get a partial office rather than set up a full office of their own. And he could charge a commission on each such transaction! With a smile on his face, and dreaming of the Jaguar he would be able to buy in just a few years, Abhishek left his friend's office and almost ran home!

Over the next few days, he spoke to a close friend, Rahul Shelke, and found him equally enthusiastic about his business idea. And together they started planning this new venture. Fixed deposits were broken, movies and entertainment were cut back on, girlfriends were politely told they were busy and, finally, the two young friends were able to scrape together a few lakhs to fund the venture.

The first step was to give the company a name, and they settled on the interesting-sounding 'MyCuteOffice'. People sniggered at this. 'No one will take you seriously,' they said, but Abhishek was adamant. 'People will remember this brand—it's so unique!' And so the company got its cute name.

Next, they had to create a website—and an app—where people could log in and either put up their office spaces for rent or hire these spaces as tenants. Essentially, MyCuteOffice became an online aggregator—or broker—for shared office spaces. Even the concept of commission was picked up from the property broker market, which charged one month's rent per transaction. However, they decided to charge only the space owner and not the tenant, since most tenants were expected to be start-ups and might not be able to pay.

Now our founders were smart and realized two things. First of all, many of the tenants were likely to take on office spaces for short periods—after all, at least some of them were likely to be start-ups and would outgrow these spaces over time. Secondly, this was a new concept. The founders were confident they could make it work, but would the office owners agree? So Abhishek and Rahul decided to take their brokerage in monthly instalments. In other words, they would charge 8 per cent of the monthly rent every month, instead of taking the entire amount up front. Of course, if someone stayed on for more than a year, that was great, because the company would keep getting its 8 per cent every month.

The next step was marketing. To get prospective tenants, the founders decided to advertise online. People searching for office space would hopefully see their ads and at least try to find out more about the concept (remember, co-working spaces were not in vogue at that time). For space owners, however, the approach was more basic. MyCuteOffice employed a salesperson who would go around to all commercial complexes in Mumbai and knock on doors. Unfortunately, this was a new concept, and most of the time this person was turned away. However, the founders did manage to get some spaces.

And so the journey began. Two young entrepreneurs with an idea, a few lakhs in the bank and loads of passion. Initially, as with all start-ups, the going was tough. The first problem, of course, was that most people had not even heard of this concept. Office owners were, quite frankly, sceptical.

'You mean I have to let a complete outsider sit in my office? What about security? And all the confidential documents we have? No way!'

Even potential tenants were not convinced. 'You mean we have to stick to the rules, regulations and timings of that office? What if we need to work late? And what if the landlord decides he has had enough and chucks me out after a month? Where do I go?'

Incidentally, even the founders had anticipated such objections—at least initially. Fortunately, there were a few brave souls (the founders could probably count them on their fingers) who took the plunge, and Abhishek and Rahul were able to conclude the first thirty-odd transactions. And then something very interesting happened. One of their first tenants was a young man named Neelay Jain. Neelay came in as a tenant but liked the concept so much that—hold your breath—he joined the two young friends as a co-founder. So now there were three young men to run the business!

But then, of course, the inevitable happened. In spite of watching every penny that they spent, their frugal funds ran out, and they needed funding. For marketing, for operations, for salaries, for the rent of their own office. In simple words, they had reached a stage where they could not survive without funding. And that's where they approached an angel network.

The Pitch

The presentation to the angel network took place in Mumbai in the winter of 2014. Present in the room were around twenty veteran members of the network, or angels. Angels they might have been, but they were all ready to grill Abhishek and pounce on anything even remotely negative.

However, right from the beginning, the angels around the table realized that they might be on to something big. All of them were from Mumbai, and they were well aware of the high rents in the city. It was true that many small companies were not able to get rented space at reasonable rates. Conversely, it was also true that several owners of office space had spare capacity and would benefit from the rent for this extra space. Even in the other metros, while rents were not as exorbitant as in Mumbai, they were still high—and, therefore, there was an opportunity. In other words, both for the landlords and the potential tenants, this was a problem waiting to be solved. Further, given the large number of spaces in these cities, and the equally large number of people wanting office space, it was a huge opportunity—which no organized player had tapped so far.

There were other issues, of course. 'What's your entry barrier?' asked one of the angels. 'What if someone else comes up with the same concept, raises a bigger round of funding than you and kills your business?' And having said this, he looked around proudly, as if to say, 'So there!'

'Actually, at this stage, we do not have any significant entry barrier,' responded Abhishek in all honesty. 'But over time, as we get more spaces listed on our website, our entry barrier will increase. Since we are a space aggregator, the more options we have for the potential tenant, the more likely he is to come to us. Anyone else starting something similar will take a lot of time to build up the number of spaces we have, and that's the competitive advantage we will have. Of course, we'll need to grow rapidly, which we should be able to, once we get funding.'

That made sense, and the angels nodded. But there was another issue. 'We need scalability,' one of the angels said. 'You need to grow rapidly to much higher levels. And I see an issue here. Like any other property broker, you would need to take the potential tenant to several offices before he can make a decision, whether positive or negative. Either way, it requires manpower—someone who can take him around. And any business that is so dependent on manpower is naturally less scalable. How do you plan to take care of this?'

Abhishek realized this was an issue. 'Yes, that's correct, but we are hoping to use technology for this. Lots of videos and photographs that the potential tenant can see. But I agree—there is a certain amount of manpower dependence in this business. We'll need to look at this problem as we go along.'

There were a few more questions, but at the end of the session, the angels were satisfied. This seemed to be a good opportunity—a niche in the office-space rental business that had not yet been tapped. And a large niche it was. The founders were all well qualified—Abhishek himself was a chartered accountant, with an additional degree in law. There were obviously several other steps to go through but, in principle, most investors were willing to invest in the company. And at the end of it all, MyCuteOffice was the proud recipient of funding worth Rs 70 lakh.

At this stage, let's hear Abhishek himself on what happened in the pitch session:

> More than the presentation, I realized what the investors were looking for was clarity of the concept. What was the problem we were trying to solve, and what was the value proposition to the customer? And my investors clearly liked the concept of being a platform for unutilized office space.
>
> I think the other thing that went in our favour was honesty. There were several questions to which we didn't have answers. Rather than guess or lie, we decided to be up front and say we didn't know. Investors realise that you will not have all the answers—especially in the early stages of the business—and are willing to live with it. But they definitely don't want to be fooled!

After the Funding

Now you can imagine the reaction of the founders once the funding was approved. That's right—they were over the moon! They finally had money in the bank! They could now put into practice all those terrific plans they had made. And that night, for the first time in months, they celebrated with beer and high-quality pao bhaji!

But even after getting the funding, progress was slow. As the investors had guessed, to conclude each deal, someone from the team had to accompany each prospective tenant to shortlisted offices, just as a regular broker would. And it took several such visits before a deal could be concluded. Several office spaces were not great and had to be knocked out of their database. And then there was the paperwork—an agreement had to be signed between the space owner and the tenant. In fact, the amount of manual effort required was huge.

It was also taking a lot of time to get both landlords and tenants to accept the concept. In fact, for the first two years, it was slow-going. After all, it was a fairly revolutionary concept and people wanted someone else to take the risk before they did. Abhishek, however, still believed that he could get business to pick up. But for that, he needed marketing spend—lots of it. And that meant money. But the company had almost run out of money and the numbers had not yet picked up sufficiently to approach VCs. And so it became a vicious cycle—no money, therefore no significant marketing, therefore no increase in business, and therefore no money!

This is what Abhishek had to say about these tough times:

> After the angel round, we got several proposals for funding, but didn't follow up on them. Perhaps we should have. We realized later on that it's important to have some funds in reserve. Ideally 50%. You never know what's going to happen, particularly in a new business, and you must have some funds to fall back on. Otherwise you run out of money and then get into a mode where you are desperately chasing money, rather than focusing on your business.

The founders had heard about this happening to many start-ups, but it was scary to have it happen to them. After all the effort they had put in! Enthusiasm began to flag. What had seemed like a great idea did not seem so great any more. Even the regular pao bhaji dinners the founders used to have became tasteless affairs—so what if beer was part of the menu?

However, Abhishek was not the kind to give up easily. He decided to move the company into survival mode. Cut costs wherever possible—including the salaries of the founders. Reduce employees and replace them with interns. Reduce salaries wherever possible and increase commissions. In other words, move away from fixed costs to variable costs—costs that would be incurred only when a transaction took place and therefore revenue came in.

Now they say that once you've reached the bottom, there is nowhere to go but up. And lo and behold, this actually began to happen. Some two years into the business, the concept started gaining acceptance. Landlords who had rented out their office spaces found it a good way to get additional income, and most of them realized it was not really a hassle. Even security was not an issue. Consequently, many of them spoke to their friends, and these friends also decided to try out the same experiment. Referrals became the name of the game. In other words, what Abhishek could not force through marketing and advertising started happening through word of mouth. Yes, it took time, but then any new concept does take time, doesn't it? Gradually, MyCuteOffice became more and more of a known name in office-property circles, and the founders realized the value of the interesting-sounding brand name. Something that people remembered.

There was something else that started happening. Now that the company had been around for more than two years, the founders had seen thousands of office spaces. In the process—and this is important, so please put down your cup of coffee and pay attention—poor-quality spaces were weeded out and only the good ones remained. Plus, the founders did something else—they asked the tenants to rate the properties they had occupied. This rating was done on the company's website or app, and tenants were happy to do so. Naturally, the poor-quality spaces were further filtered out. As a result, Abhishek realized that, in many cases, they actually did not need to accompany the potential tenant when he or she visited an office space, because most spaces that remained after the filtering were good anyway. And, in any case, by now MyCuteOffice had built something of a positive reputation for quality spaces, so tenants were willing to take out the time and visit these office spaces on their own.

And this had huge implications for the company. Suddenly, the manual intervention needed to close a deal reduced. Which meant less manpower or, conversely, more business with the same manpower. In other words, salaries and conveyance took up a lesser percentage of the revenue. The business became more scalable—which was one of the concerns that the angels had. Quite naturally, there was more money left to spend on marketing and expanding the business. You can imagine the rest. Numbers grew, as did the brand.

By the way, we almost forgot. There was another interesting risk to the business that we hadn't mentioned earlier. Remember, the commission to the company was being paid on a monthly basis. Now after the first month, what if the landlord were to turn around and say, 'Thank you, Abhishek. I don't need you any more. I'll take the monthly rent directly from the tenant, so I don't need to pay you.' You see the risk, don't you?

However, that did not happen. By this time, landlords had realized that they needed MyCuteOffice as much as MyCuteOffice needed them. Since their tenants typically stayed on for only a few months, they would need to get another tenant once the earlier one left. And where would they get this new tenant? MyCuteOffice, of course! In other words, it became a long-term partnership between landlords and Abhishek's company, and very few landlords bypassed them.

Now, in 2017, something really, really important happened. As you are aware, by this time, co-working spaces had become relatively common, and the bright young Abhishek sensed another opportunity for growing the business. Rather than looking at just unoccupied parts of existing offices, he started identifying fully vacant office spaces. He would then meet the owner and propose a partnership, in which the *entire space* would be converted into a co-working space, jointly branded between the owner and MyCuteOffice. The investments in the office space would come from the owner, and Abhishek and his team would manage and market it. In other words, *MyCuteOffice had moved from being a pure aggregator of shared office spaces to co-branding and managing co-working spaces.*

In fact, he went a step further. He realized that most existing co-working spaces, such as WeWork, 91springboard and Awfis, were expensive. Many small companies and start-ups would not be able to afford the rent they charged. And so he put on his thinking cap again. Could co-working spaces be made more affordable? For instance, did they really need huge, lavish reception areas? Did they need large, free spaces for occupants to move around and possibly chat in? Most importantly, were tenants willing to pay significantly higher rents for these 'perks'? Or was there a sizeable population that wanted well-located, clean, comfortable but functional areas which took care of their needs—sufficient but not excessive free space, enough storage, tea and coffee percolators, a refrigerator, a microwave oven, etc.

Smart guy that he was, Abhishek brought in an architect who helped optimize each potential co-working space—maximize seats and, at the same time, ensure comfort. Effectively, Abhishek had created a new paradigm in co-working spaces—namely *affordable co-working spaces.* Interestingly, the rental charged per seat was at least 40 per cent lower than that charged by the large, expensive co-working spaces in the same localities. Our friend Abhishek had effectively created a kind of OYO Rooms for office space. And looking at the phenomenal growth OYO Rooms has seen, you can imagine the potential growth of MyCuteOffice.

Obviously, this would not have worked three years earlier, when co-working was a nascent concept. But now landlords with empty spaces lapped it up and at the time of writing, Abhishek had already signed up and launched five such co-working spaces in Mumbai, in addition to the shared spaces that he already had. Importantly, the company remains profitable. And with the profitability challenges faced by some of the larger players in the business, who knows? In the long run, perhaps it'll be Abhishek's model that the others would adopt.

And now a note for you, dear reader. If you happen to live in Mumbai and go to Kandivali, and by a strange coincidence if you happen to land up at Abhishek's office, you will see a very, very busy but happy young man. And if you were to stay long enough to see him take a well-deserved break, you may see him gazing into the distance, thinking of Bengaluru, Hyderabad, even Dubai and Singapore, where he could spread his wings . . .

So let's leave Abhishek with his dreams.

Analysis

So that was the cute story of MyCuteOffice. But, in life, it's not just enough to read stories. You also need to learn something from them. Let's now analyse what happened, what the angel investors were thinking and why they decided to invest in the company. Remember the PERSISTENT approach we had talked about in the Introduction? As we had mentioned, successful businesses follow the PERSISTENT approach. And therefore investors look for such start-ups to fund.

So what is the PERSISTENT approach that Abhishek followed? Good question.

First of all, there was a clear PROBLEM that Abhishek was solving—that of providing low-cost, shared office spaces to companies. Even landlords got a bonus—rents that they never expected. Equally important, they were willing to pay for it. And that's the 'P' in PERSISTENT.

Next, we have the first 'S' in PERSISTENT, namely SIZE OF THE MARKET. Why is this important? Obvious, isn't it? The whole purpose of creating a start-up is to ultimately create a giant. Sure, you may be an exception and are desperate to create a small, stagnant start-up, but then you'd be in a ridiculously small minority, wouldn't you? And how can you create a giant if the market itself is small? And therefore SIZE OF THE MARKET becomes critical. Fortunately for MyCuteOffice, office rental was a huge market, even if they were to stick to Mumbai alone. Of course, if they were to expand to other cities, it would be far larger. And that made it an even more attractive business.

When you get investors on board, SIZE OF THE MARKET becomes even more critical. Look at it this way. You are looking at your venture as your baby—hopefully for life. But the investor who has put in money wants returns, and that, too, reasonably fast. Now he can get returns only when some other investor buys out his shares at a higher valuation. That investor, too, expects a third investor to buy out his shares, and so on. And all this can only happen if the SIZE OF THE MARKET is truly large. Otherwise very soon this cycle will stop, because fresh investors do not see significant growth any more. Get the idea?

Now we're sure you have a question. And you're right, it's a very relevant question. What's the point of a huge market if your business does not SCALE up rapidly within this market? Let's also take a look at the investor's point of view. Risks in a start-up are clearly high. It's an unproven company, and it may or may not survive. And when an investor buys shares in the company, he cannot sell them in the stock market simply because they are not listed. He can only sell them when someone else—usually another investor—is willing to invest in the company, and therefore buys his shares. So the risks are far higher, and the shares are illiquid. Quite naturally, therefore, an investor putting money into a start-up wants much higher returns than he would get in the stock market, and that, too, consistently over several years. Which means the business needs to grow rapidly to a very large size. For this to happen, we have already seen that SIZE OF THE MARKET is critical. But in addition, the business needs to be able to SCALE up rapidly within this market for investors to be interested. So that's the second 'S' in PERSISTENT, namely SCALABILITY.

Now here's what happened to SCALABILITY in Abhishek's case. In the beginning, he had to have one of his people accompanying the tenant when he visited possible spaces. In other words, some employee would have to make multiple visits before a deal was signed—and in some cases, no deal was signed. A lot of manual involvement. Importantly, *any business that has too much manual involvement is tough to scale*. Because then, for any growth in your business, you will need to add a proportionate number of people. Over time, however, as the poor-quality spaces got filtered out, the need for an employee to accompany the tenant came down. So the business became more and more SCALABLE. Voila!

Let's summarize. Any business needs to solve a PROBLEM, where the MARKET SIZE is large and the business model is SCALABLE. That much is clear. But can they do so profitably? Are the EARNINGS positive? Or at least, is there a possibility of the EARNINGS becoming positive in future? If the business is inherently loss-making, it will always be dependent on funding, even for survival. And that simply won't do! So let's look at the EARNINGS MODEL—the first 'E' in our PERSISTENT approach. There are obviously two components to EARNINGS. One is revenue and the other is costs. Abhishek was getting revenue from commissions and later from processing charges as well, so the revenue part of the model was fine. But what about costs?

Now here we need to introduce an interesting term, namely *unit economics*. Which simply means *earnings or profitability at the level of each unit*. What is a unit, you might ask? Actually that's not a very easy question to answer, so let's simply define it for the original shared office model of MyCuteOffice. In simple terms, a unit in MyCuteOffice could be one transaction—in other words, one rental contract between a tenant and a space owner. *The revenue earned from this transaction minus the direct*

cost of executing the transaction gives you the earnings at the unit
level. In this case, the revenue was clear—it was the commission
earned. The costs could include the running around to complete
the transaction, the paperwork, the legal fees, if any, etc. It would
not include overheads such as marketing and salaries. Clearly, the
cost of executing a transaction was not significant, and therefore
this business was profitable at the unit level. In other words,
the unit economics was positive.

And this is key—at the very least, any business needs to have
positive EARNINGS at the level of the unit. If not, the more
transactions you have, the more you lose. And when overheads
are added to that, the business can never make a profit. It can never
be viable. However, if the unit economics of a business is positive,
there is a chance that EARNINGS will be positive at the level of
the company. At least somewhere in the future, when the volumes
are large enough and the sum of the EARNINGS from each unit is
greater than the overheads of the business.

If that is clear, let's take a look at the investor's viewpoint.
At an early stage in any business, volumes are low and, therefore, the
overall business is unlikely to be profitable. Moreover, it is virtually
impossible to predict the kind of marketing spend required to make
the business profitable as a whole. And, therefore, angels would not
use this as a decision point. But—and this is an extremely important
'but'—the unit economics of the business needs to be positive.
Of course, you may start by selling at a discount, so as to rapidly
grow your customer base. In this case, the unit economics may be
negative, to start with. But at some stage, it will need to become
positive for the business to be viable, and therefore for the investor
to become interested. In the case of MyCuteOffice, it was clearly
positive, which was fine for the angels around the table.

Now you are probably thinking that this is a ridiculously
simple concept, and you've mastered it by now. However, life—
and business—can never be so simple. Let's ask you a question:
Is this the only way we can define a unit for MyCuteOffice?

Suppose, instead, that we move towards their current model, where they manage branded co-working spaces. And we consider one full co-working space to be one unit. We would now need to look at the average revenue we can get from this space per month, which means we bring in issues of occupancy. So we now have a new definition of 'unit economics', and therefore a new level of profitability. But our earlier comment still stands. Irrespective of how you define your unit, it must be profitable—otherwise it cannot be viable once you add overheads.

Now for the extremely important 'R' in PERSISTENT, namely RISKS to the business. What were the RISKS faced by Abhishek and gang? Well, there was the obvious RISK of the market not accepting their offering. So landlords might have been unwilling to have unknown people on their premises for security reasons. Conversely, tenants might not have wanted to comply with any restrictions that landlords might impose. For instance, tenants might have wanted to work late but landlords would perhaps not be willing. There was the added risk of landlords and tenants doing a side deal after a month and bypassing the company, thereby knocking out the commission that MyCuteOffice would have earned. You see? Founders as well as investors need to be aware of the RISKS the company faces, and how they plan to mitigate them. Fortunately, in the case of our young friend Abhishek, both the RISKS mentioned above came down with time and, in fact, vanished once he moved into the co-working model. Incidentally, most founders tend to overlook RISKS, assuming that things will go well. It's always a good idea to discuss the business with friends and get them to poke holes in your model—in other words, to try and come up with potential RISKS that can kill the business. After all, it's better to be prepared in advance, isn't it?

By the way, one standard RISK faced by every company—whether start-up or behemoth—is competition. Could MyCuteOffice remain ahead of competitors? And what if a new competitor—perhaps with deeper pockets—were to enter the market? We are all aware that office rental is an extremely crowded space—with brokers lurking in every corner of Mumbai. And investors are smart. They definitely do not want to invest in a crowded space with lots of competitors. So what do they look for? A NICHE within this crowded space, quite naturally. More specifically, a large enough NICHE, which, therefore, permits the business to scale up. In this case, MyCuteOffice had discovered a large, untapped NICHE, because shared office space was a new concept and brokers were not yet into this business. And that's the 'N' in PERSISTENT. Incidentally, using shared spaces was also a highly INNOVATIVE solution—which gives us the 'I' in PERSISTENT.

In general, to overcome the threat of current as well as future competition, every business needs what we call an ENTRY BARRIER—the second 'E' in PERSISTENT. Sometimes also called 'competitive advantage'. As you might have guessed, an ENTRY BARRIER makes it difficult for a competitor to enter your business. In the case of MyCuteOffice, initially there was no such barrier. But over time, Abhishek built up a large database of office spaces, which gave him a significant advantage over any new competitor. Any potential tenant would rather come to a broker who had a large number of options than to someone who had just a few. So that would make it tougher for a competitor to enter. In fact, as MyCuteOffice expanded in the future, the database would only grow larger, making the ENTRY BARRIER even stronger.

While on the subject of RISKS, we need to mention one RISK that all start-ups face. A RISK that is the basis for this book. Namely, the possibility of funding not coming in when required. And for this, it is always desirable to have a back-up business plan. In case things work out well and you get your funding, go ahead and use your regular high-growth plan. Which will probably include hiring people, large marketing spends and so on. Hopefully, as you implement this plan, you will grow rapidly. But in case the funding doesn't materialize, you would need to cut your costs and prepare for the long haul. And that's where you would need to move to your back-up plan—also called a survival plan. Cut your costs and try and move fixed costs to variable ones. For instance, reduce salaries and increase commissions, replace employees with interns, use referral policies instead of marketing spend. Remain at break-even so that you can survive for a few months, by which time you'll hopefully get your funding, or your business picks up. And as you would have noticed, that's exactly what MyCuteOffice did.

And then, of course, there is the first 'T' in PERSISTENT—the TEAM, starting with the founders. Perhaps the most important thing that any investor looks for. In fact, in early-stage start-ups, many investors look more at the founders than at the business. Why? Simply because at such an early stage, no one has any idea what direction the business will ultimately take. But if they have the right founders, these founders will pivot as required and make the business a success—which did happen in this case, when Abhishek and gang moved to co-working spaces. In addition, Abhishek and his partners exuded both conviction and passion. Most importantly, they were honest. Where they did not know the answer, they said so quite truthfully. And the angels were convinced.

All this is great, but isn't there something we have missed? The investor would look at market size, entry barriers, scalability and all the other terms we have discussed, but at the end of the day, isn't there something else he would look at too?

Of course there is. Investors do not invest in bright ideas alone. They want proof. They want to see if all the above good things have actually led to customers coming in. And more and more of them coming in over time. Ideally bringing in revenue—although some ventures do not have revenue, at least initially. And that, ladies and gentlemen, is what we call TRACTION—the last 'T' in PERSISTENT. The culmination of all that's good about the business, which the investor wants to see before he puts his hard-earned money into the venture. In the case of Abhishek, at the time of asking for funding, there were a few spaces he had lined up and a few transactions completed. So there wasn't much TRACTION. However, the investors believed in the story and were therefore willing to put their money into the company.

In general, however, you must remember that most investors look for proof that the idea is actually working on the ground. And the only way they can check for this is TRACTION, isn't it? So a good time to go in for funding is when you have been able to show sufficient TRACTION.

And that, my friend, is the PERSISTENT model that both start-ups as well as investors look at.

The Impact of the Coronavirus—or Any Other Crisis

What do you do when such an unprecedented crisis hits you? It could be the COVID-19 crisis, or the global financial crisis of 2008 or, for that matter, any crisis that may appear in the future. Well, as you can imagine, money becomes more scarce in these conditions and investors become very, very choosy. They look for even more PERSISTENT start-ups to invest in. And that is what your start-up needs to be.

But there's something more. Remember, Abhishek faced exactly the same problem some time back, where he wasn't getting funding. And what did he do? Simple. He cut costs drastically and went into survival mode. Thereby he was able to last through the tough period. And that's exactly what you need to do. Cut unnecessary costs—especially fixed costs. Reduce salaries where possible, and move to variable compensation. Reduce marketing expenses. Give up unnecessary office spaces if you can. Keep your company ticking and move from growth mode to survival mode. During such times, many others will fall by the wayside. And if you've survived, well, once funding comes back into the market, you're in business!

Finally, here is a table that captures the essence of the approach, as applied to MyCuteOffice:

The PERSISTENT Approach Applied to MyCuteOffice

	Issue	MyCuteOffice
P	**PROBLEM:** Are you solving a real problem? Will people pay?	Low-cost rented office space. Additional rent for the space owner.
E	**EARNINGS MODEL**	Revenues from commissions. Unit economics positive.
R	**RISKS** and how you will mitigate them	Would space owners be comfortable? Could the space owner and tenant bypass MyCuteOffice after a month? Both risks mitigated over time.
S	**SIZE OF THE MARKET**	Very large. Expandable to all metros.
I	**INNOVATION**	Making use of spare office space.
S	**SCALABILITY**	Not scalable initially, because of manual intervention. Scalability improved as manual intervention went down with time.
T	**TEAM,** starting with the founders	High conviction and passion. Sincere and honest founders.
E	**ENTRY BARRIERS**	Initially none. Over time, the brand and the growing database of spaces.
N	**NICHE:** When the market is crowded, identify a niche	Office-space aggregation is a crowded sector. But shared office space creates a potentially large niche.
T	**TRACTION**	Some limited traction at the time of the fund raise—thirty-plus spaces listed and just over ten transactions.

One last word. Apart from the acronym PERSISTENT, what is extremely, extremely important is the English word 'persistent'. When you have a start-up, things will go wrong, many assumptions that you made will be invalid, funds will dry up and competition will heat up—along with your stress levels and blood pressure, of course. These are just a few of the things that can go wrong. But, dear founder, you need to persevere. And after that, you need to persevere some more. And more. Patience is the name of the game. That's what Abhishek and his team did—and they succeeded. And that's the crux of starting and running a business, isn't it?

4

SQRRL Away, Save and Invest[*]

Have you ever sat in a park and watched squirrels in action? Try it sometime—you'll find it extremely relaxing. And if you have, you would have noticed that these cute little creatures locate small nuts and berries. Some of them are eaten, but, most importantly, others are stored away for a rainy day. One by tiny one. In the process, the squirrel actually builds up a large 'corpus' of nuts and other edible items.

Fascinating though squirrels can be, we need to move away and focus on start-ups. Specifically on an interesting person called Samant Sikka. Samant was a senior vice president at Axis Bank and an investment adviser to his clients. In other words, his job was to help clients save and invest money. One day, he was sitting in a park near his house and doing precisely what we have discussed above—watching squirrels in action. Suddenly he sat bolt upright—and scared away the squirrels in the process. Weren't the squirrels doing exactly what he asked his clients to do? Saving small amounts bit by bit and ultimately building a large corpus?

---

[*] Taken from the authors' personal interviews with Samant Sikka between 2018 and 2020.

That was the time Samant decided that he would form his own company, which would do precisely this—help clients 'squirrel away' small amounts of money, and thereby grow the corpus over time. He spoke to a couple of friends who were as excited as he was, and agreed to become co-founders. Quite naturally, the company was to be called SQUIRREL, but he ultimately plumped for the shorter and more interesting SQRRL (he was a bit averse to vowels, you see).

Now if you are a normal human being (sometimes we do need to make such baseless assumptions), you would agree that saving is a very tough thing to do. There are just so many terrific spending opportunities around you that you never get down to saving. Or perhaps you are abnormal and do manage to save, but inertia prevents you from doing it too often. Too much hassle. You may do it a couple of times but it ends there. And that, dear reader, was the barrier Samant and his colleagues needed to overcome. Getting people to save on a regular basis. Something that was most unnatural for most human beings.

So how did they do it? For the answer to this question, let's take you back to your grandmother's days. Now, in those days, most women did not work—or rather, they did work at home but did not get paid for it. So your grandmother did not get a salary. But she did get money from your grandfather for household expenses. Very likely she would keep what was called a *gullak*, or piggy bank. A small, round earthen container—usually striped—with a slot for putting in coins. Now, every time she spent some money on buying vegetables or milk or whatever she had to buy, she would get back some change. And this is the crucial bit—a small part of this change would be put away in the gullak—perhaps as little as 25 paise or even 10 paise. That's it. Every purchase would lead to one or two coins going into her 'corpus'. Importantly, she could not take this money out unless she broke the gullak. And therefore, the corpus got built over time.

Now please note something very, very important. This approach to saving was entirely painless, simply because the amounts involved were small. She might have spent, say, Rs 12 on vegetables and

10 paise extra didn't really hurt. And that, ladies and gentlemen, was the key to Samant's thinking. He had to make the process of saving painless. So if you spent Rs 680 and this was rounded off to Rs 700, it wouldn't hurt you—just as the 10 paise didn't hurt your grandmother. And this extra Rs 20 would be saved. Now if you've understood this concept, you've just understood Samant's offering!

How does it work? Well, you are aware that every time you make a purchase—which can be through a credit card, a debit card, netbanking or even by cheque—you get an SMS on your phone. SQRRL then accesses this SMS and extracts the amount you have spent in this transaction. At the end of the day—or week, depending on what you prefer—these amounts are added up, and SQRRL rounds this up to the next hundred. This 'rounded-up amount' is then SQRRLed away and added to your corpus. As an example, if you have spent Rs 754 during the day, SQRRL rounds it up to Rs 800, and this additional Rs 46 is then SQRRLed away.

Of course, there are a couple of caveats. When you sign up for this service, SQRRL has to be given permission to access your SMSs—and it doesn't pick up anything other than financial transactions. Definitely not messages from your girlfriend or boyfriend. Secondly, you could specify an upper limit per week or per month so that you don't go bankrupt!

Aha. Can you now see one major benefit of Samant's approach over your grandmother's? Sure you can—*here, the squirreling away is done automatically.* You do not have to remember to save those titbits every time. They are automatically saved, simply because you have given instructions to your friendly SQRRL gullak to save the amounts at the end of every day or week.

And, by the way, what do you think Samant called this offering? Guess?

SQRRLAWAY, of course!

Now, here it is important to understand Samant's thought process. Who was his target audience? Samant was very, very clear. He was looking at young people. Those who had not yet got into the habit of saving and investing. After all, older people would perhaps already be into some kind of monthly savings through SIPs (systematic investment plans), which are offered by all mutual funds. Samant realized that he would find it tough to get such people to switch to his offering. And, therefore, he was attempting to tap young people *before they had got into such investments.* Essentially college students and young professionals. So that he could inculcate the savings habit in them at an early age, when they were not thinking about SIPs. And perhaps hadn't even heard of them. He realized, rightly, that he needed to 'catch them young' and then make them customers for life.

So you have now understood the critical part of Samant's offering—namely the automatic and painless saving. And now we come to the other equally important part—this corpus that was getting created incrementally needed to be invested, so as to give some returns on the savings. Unlike your grandmother's gullak, where 10 paise would remain 10 paise, Samant had to ensure that you got some returns on your savings, and therefore the corpus grew. Now here you must appreciate the thinking of the young person who had begun his or her savings habit with SQRRLAWAY. What if the corpus was to be invested in the stock market? Sure, the returns were likely to be high. But what if Donald Trump were to initiate yet another trade war with China, and therefore the stock market tanked? Or the United Kingdom decided to get into Brexit mode again, and once again the market tanked? Or a war were to break out between Upper Lamaria and Lower Lamaria, and therefore world trade collapsed, once again sending the stock market crashing (by the way, we are not sure if Lamaria is a real country, but it sounds like one, doesn't it)? Anyhow, to get back to SQRRL, Samant could use all his persuasive skills to try and convince the young saver that the two Lamarias would kiss and make up, and therefore the stock market would ultimately revive, but would that convince the saver? For perhaps the first time in his life, the saver had started saving, and suddenly, due to events in the US or the UK or Upper Lamaria, or anywhere else in the world, his savings had crashed. *And he was left with less than he had put in in the first place.* Would SQRRL ever be able to convince this young person to persist with his habit of saving? Of course not. He would probably leave immediately, use a few choice swear words for SQRRL (which we cannot reproduce in this book for obvious reasons), and also get his friends to leave.

Now, Samant was smart. And he realized early on that he could not take a risk with the money put in by first-time savers. So rather than expose them to the ups and downs of the stock market, he decided to offer them something simple and safe. Liquid funds. Easy for customers to understand, with better returns than a savings bank account and, above all, non-volatile. All amounts SQRRLed away from a customer were invested in liquid funds. And if you are aware of what these are, you would know that they are safe, in the sense that they do not tank. And they give you returns every day—even though these returns are very small. Typically an annualized return of around 6–7 per cent, similar to fixed deposits. But they are returns all the same, and the important thing is that the saver could actually see his corpus growing every day, thanks to the liquid fund. Even better, he could ask for his corpus back whenever he wanted. And so Samant was able to add the icing on the cake for the saver—even though it was a very thin layer of icing. In the process, he believed that he could get the first-time saver to gain confidence in SQRRL and therefore get hooked to the habit of saving.

Having got several young people hooked, Samant was now ready to take them to the next level—and therefore to his next product. That of goal-based investing. Here SQRRL would start by getting you to define your goal—which could be a foreign trip, or a car, or that heavenly motorbike which your girlfriend was dead gone on (and the one her other potential boyfriend was planning to buy). Along with your time frames for this goal. And one more critical piece of the puzzle—namely the levels of risk you were willing to take. Based on these inputs, SQRRL would do asset allocation for you appropriately.

Does this sound like Greek? Or Hebrew? Okay, let's take a simple example. Suppose you wanted to give yourself a foreign holiday in two years. So that was your goal as well as the time frame. Now if you were a risk-averse person, you might have to put in, say, Rs 10,000 every month, which would be invested in some debt fund—giving you returns of, say, 7 per cent minus tax, and with that you could manage. But if you were willing to take a short-term risk, you might need to put away only Rs 8,000 every month, and this would be invested in the stock market—through equity mutual funds—which could give you 12–15 per cent returns per year. So with this higher risk, you would need to put in less every month to reach the same goal within the same time frame. Obviously, the higher risk meant that if the stock market crashed, your corpus would actually come down and you would not be able to ski in Switzerland, or play with giraffes in Namibia, or whatever it is that you wanted to do. Of course, in the long run, you would recover your losses and make much more than you would with a debt fund, but your vacation would be pushed into the future. But that's the meaning of risk, isn't it?

As with the rest of his business model, Samant was clear that the keyword here was simplicity. Most of his customers were unlikely to be interested in the complexities of investing. If he were to bring in terms such as NAV (net asset value) or alpha or beta or price-to-earnings ratio, the effect on the customer was likely to be, 'Too complex for me. I don't want to get into all this.' So Samant simplified the whole business of investing by creating three categories of savings—high risk, medium risk and low risk. But that still sounded complex, so he cleverly branded them as 'Adventurous', 'Practical' and 'Cautious' portfolios. That's it. If you chose the Adventurous portfolio, your money would be invested largely in the stock market through mutual funds. For the Practical portfolio, it would be a combination of stocks and debt funds. And for the Cautious types, it would be entirely debt funds. And of course, given that he was dealing with young customers, the obvious interface for them was an app, which he developed, along with his team.

Simple, isn't it? Define your goals and time frames, specify your risk levels, and SQRRL would help you figure out how much you needed to put away every month, and where. All through an easy-to-use app.

So that was Samant's brilliant concept—getting people to save, and subsequently invest. But, of course, you are aware that every business will have competition lurking around the corner. Now Samant's initial offering—SQRRLAWAY—was rather unique. Yes, there were a few small-time players doing something similar to encourage people to save, but there was no biggie in the business. However, for the second product, namely goal-based investing, he was competing with literally an army of agents selling mutual funds. Agents who anyway exhorted people to invest small amounts regularly—through SIPs. Which essentially is what his goal-based investment product was. So how could Samant hope to compete in such a crowded space? How was he different, and therefore how could he get his customers to invest through SQRRL, rather than leave and invest through the many, many other agents lurking around?

Well, first of all, Samant was 'catching them young'. Most of his customers were college students or young adults who had not got into the SIP culture as yet. Hopefully, with SQRRLAWAY, they would have built some level of trust in the company. Because of which they were likely to buy their mutual funds through SQRRL, rather than through some other agent. It wasn't guaranteed, of course, but it was likely. Next, notice what Samant was doing. He wasn't just selling mutual funds. He was actually doing some level of financial planning for his customers. The kind that financial advisers would do for more wealthy guys. The regular agent selling mutual funds would simply ask the investor to start an SIP of, say, Rs 5,000 in some specific mutual fund. Which was largely an arbitrary piece of advice. But Samant was doing much more. He was asking his customers to define their goals, time frames and risk levels. How much they would need to invest every month and where would be decided based on these inputs. Samant had actually made SQRRL into a simple, basic-level financial adviser for his young clients, which typical agents were definitely not. And that, ladies and gentlemen, is why he stood out from the crowd.

Finally, we come to a very, very important question—what about revenues? Sure, through SQRRLAWAY he was able to enrol young adults and get them into the habit of saving painlessly. In that sense, he was solving a real problem. But would people pay for this? Maybe, or maybe not. And if they were asked to pay, the numbers he could enrol would probably reduce dramatically. Further, in the goal-based investing option, he was helping them plan and achieve their goals. Once again, would people pay? Unlikely. However, by now you must have realized that Samant was a smart entrepreneur. He had decided that revenues were not really his immediate priority. His priority was to catch lots and lots of young men and women, and get them into the habit of saving through an automatic, painless process. Hopefully, these customers would stay with him for life, or at least for a long, long time. And there would be lots of opportunities to offer other products and services to these customers over time—such as share trading, financial advisory services, sale of insurance products, etc. For which he could charge a fee. By the way, if you have noticed, this strategy is very similar to what some other smart people (such as Mark Zuckerberg) had adopted in the past. Get lots of customers hooked, make it a habit and only then focus on revenue.

The Fund Raise and After

A few months into the project, the founders decided to raise funds. Now their fund raise was a little different from what you've seen with MyCuteOffice, so you need to wake up and read carefully. Wash your face if that helps. This was a B2C business, with no immediate revenues. Revenues would only come in the future. At the same time, it was vital to grow rapidly and have a large base of excited and hopefully loyal users. Which meant major marketing spends. Also, Samant would need to build a completely automated system, which would include a smooth, easy-to-use interface for the users. So he would also require funds for product development. In other words, the company was in a position where it was unlikely to get any significant revenues in the foreseeable future but at the same time it would require large funding. In fact, about a million dollars (around Rs 7 crore, for those of you who are too lazy to do currency conversion).

Clearly, this was a major challenge. Samant and his colleagues realized that most angel networks would not be able to arrange this kind of funding. So what did they do? Obvious, isn't it? They simply skipped the angel stage and went directly to a VC. Happily, it worked. The VC was impressed with the founders—senior professionals with just the right kind of experience. They also liked the concept. And what really worked in their favour was that the founders had walked away from successful corporate careers and invested a large chunk of their personal savings in the venture. Which spoke volumes about their commitment. As a consequence, SQRRL was able to raise its first investment of a million dollars from an early-stage VC fund!

At this point, it's interesting to hear what Samant has to say on the subject of fundraising:

> There is too much hype in the media about funding. It seems to have become a kind of validation of the business model, as well as the team. So instead of focusing on the business, many entrepreneurs get distracted and spend unnecessary time and effort on fundraising. Which has huge ramifications in the long run. The really tough job for founders is to strike a balance between business growth and fundraising.
>
> Incidentally, fundraising is a double-edged sword. You must remember that a VC is a fund manager who has taken money from investors for a fixed time period—say five years. At the end of this period, the money needs to be returned to the investors, hopefully with significant gains. And that means the VC needs an exit. So by design, the start-up is expected to

give the VC such an exit. And that's the trap the entrepreneur can fall into—where he is *building to sell* rather than building a great business, as was true in the good old days. You cannot build to sell. Build a great business—if, along the way, you get an opportunity to sell some stake, maybe you could. But your aim should not be building to sell.

Fortunately, the VC from whom we raised money was completely aligned with our vision and backed the team. And that's my advice to all young friends reading this book. Choose your investor carefully. The investor's thinking must be completely aligned with yours. They should be a partner in the business rather than just an investor. I would go as far as to say, 'Who you take the money from is as important as the money itself. Don't take the money if it comes from the wrong investor. It can be a pain.'

As you can imagine, the money Samant raised helped him to grow the business. At the time of writing this book, he had well over three lakh SQRRL savers cum investors on board. And the number is growing rapidly every month. Incidentally, now that he has these customers, he has started offering them paid services such as insurance products as well. Yes, dear reader, Samant is very much on the way to realizing his ambition—of becoming a giant in the financial services business.

And by the way, if you were to check out the business channels on television, you might just catch Samant advising young investors on the concept of SQRRLing. We strongly suggest you tune in. And we can guarantee that you'll benefit from it.

Analysis

Most of this analysis is obvious, so we'll leave it to you—definitely a PROBLEM waiting to be solved, a very large MARKET SIZE, a highly SCALABLE business, a great TEAM led by founders with just the right experience, catching customers young before they get hooked to the SIP mutual funds bandwagon, and hopefully retaining them for life . . .

But there is one issue that we must discuss, because that goes strongly against our PERSISTENT model. Yes, there was a PROBLEM, and Samant had worked out a terrific solution to it, but the key question is, 'Would customers pay?' Aha. Most likely not. Because investing in mutual funds—which is what Samant was ultimately doing on behalf of his customers—is free. So why would customers pay? In other words, did he have an EARNINGS MODEL?

Samant was very clear that he *did not want his customers to pay*. At least not right away. He simply wanted them to sign up, get hooked and make saving, and therefore investing, a habit. And he wanted lots of these customers. Over time, he could get revenues out of them through other paid products—which he was able to. Or use advertising to generate revenues—rather like his illustrious predecessors Facebook and Google. So in the long run, he expected to get revenues, but in the short term, he simply wanted to maximize his loyal customer base. Crucially, he was able to convince a VC about his thinking—numbers first and revenues later. And that's how he got his money.

That's an interesting thought to end this story on. You may not be earning revenues right now. But if you are adding a large number of 'sticky' customers who can give you revenues in future, that's fine. Investors will buy into the idea. Just remember that you will need a large amount of funding—possibly multiple rounds—before your revenues kick in. So yours would not be a typical angel-investor story. You'll need some big angels—the real HNI variety—or a VC fund, for this kind of fund raise.

The Impact of the Coronavirus—or Any Other Crisis

While the COVID-19 crisis has made things tougher for everyone, at least in the short term, just look at the opportunity it has opened up for a company like SQRRL. You would agree that habits will change and people will spend more time at home—at least in the short to medium term. They are less likely to go to their friendly neighbourhood agent to buy mutual funds or insurance policies. That's where a business such as SQRRL can benefit. And that's where you, dear founder, can benefit as well. If your business is largely online, you have a better chance of getting funding. If it's not online, well, pivot your business so that at least part of it goes online. And therefore enhance your chances of getting funding.

Finally, what does our PERSISTENT table look like?

The PERSISTENT Approach Applied to SQRRL

	Issue	SQRRL
P	**PROBLEM:** Are you solving a real problem? Will people pay?	Yes—the problem of saving and investing regularly and painlessly. People would not have to pay right now. However, over time, paid products could be offered to customers.
E	**EARNINGS MODEL**	No immediate earnings model. Focus on acquiring a large pool of customers, and then getting revenues over time.
R	**RISKS** and how you will mitigate them	Major delays in getting revenues and lack of funding to tide over this period.
S	**SIZE OF THE MARKET**	Very large. India has perhaps the largest bunch of millennials in the world.
I	**INNOVATION**	The painless SQRRLAWAY approach to regular saving.
S	**SCALABILITY**	Very high. Large, underserved, digitally savvy consumer base. Addressing newer segments by using vernacular languages to aid adoption.
T	**TEAM**, starting with the founders	Highly experienced, passionate, confident and knowledgeable founders.
E	**ENTRY BARRIERS**	Over time, the brand, and the sticky (and hopefully trusting) customer base.
N	**NICHE:** When the market is crowded, identify a niche	Micro-investing as against typical SIPs, which take in much larger amounts.
T	**TRACTION**	A large base of more than a lakh savers had been built by the time SQRRL went for its fund raise.

5

Recruiting Freshers with Greymeter[*]

Dear budding entrepreneur, have you ever tried to recruit freshers? If you haven't, we'd like to share the experience of a young HR executive from a software company. Incidentally, it could easily be a company in a different field—we've just taken software as an example. And let's assume that she has 400 résumés, from which she needs to recruit twenty programmers. First of all, she needs to figure out which of these candidates to shortlist for the preliminary interview. The question is, by looking at the résumés, how do you figure out who the good programmers are? Are they the ones with the best grades? Not necessarily. Are they the ones who have done the largest number of software projects? Once again, not necessarily. So what is the criteria for shortlisting these youngsters?

Tough question, isn't it? And it becomes even tougher when you extend the logic to jobs in sales or operations, or other such jobs that do not require any academic inputs. Now, our young friend would obviously not want to miss out on good candidates, so she plays it safe and shortlists 200—the ones with the best grades.

---

[*] Taken from the authors' personal interviews with Aman Garg between 2015 and 2020.

Was that the right decision? We don't know, but let's take the story further. These 200 candidates will now need to go through a preliminary interview. Assuming half an hour per interview, that makes it a hundred hours, or about fifteen days spent by perhaps two people—one from HR and one with a technical background. And what have we got at the end of this process? Further shortlisted candidates who still need to go through a couple of more rounds. What a criminal waste of time!

Ladies and gentlemen, with this build-up you begin to realize what Aman Garg was thinking when he launched Greymeter. Aman realized that this was a major problem most recruiters faced, which naturally meant that it was a major opportunity. What if he were to test the programming skills of freshers, before putting them up to companies for recruitment? What a tremendous saving of time it would be! And surely companies would be willing to pay him for this service.

The more Aman thought about it, the more he warmed to the idea. This was brilliant. He could actually test skill levels in different programming languages such as Java, C++ and Python. And then recruiters would get candidates with skills in whichever language they wanted. In fact, he could go far beyond programming. He could check out written as well as verbal communication levels for companies wanting these skills—perhaps for their sales or customer-support executives. He could also ask freshers wanting a sales executive's job to conduct a short market survey, based on which he could shortlist them. Aman began to think big. He saw himself as the pioneer in entry-level recruitment in the country. He could even go international. Companies would be queuing up for his services. He even figured out which five-star hotel he would have his office in. The dream became more and more real . . .

And then he came down to earth. First of all, he needed partners. For which he spoke to four of his classmates from college. Fortunately, they were equally excited. So with a lot of fanfare, including the inevitable guzzling of beer accompanied by a combination of chicken and paneer tikkas, Greymeter was born.

The Next Steps

The first thing to do was to figure out how they would test skill levels. The founders were clear that they were in an online business— that was the only way in which they could scale up rapidly, even into towns where they did not exist. Now checking a candidate's programming skills was relatively easy. They simply put up short programming assignments on their portal and asked him to write programs for them. And, at least initially, the grading would be done by one of the Greymeter team members. However, over time, in the interest of scalability, they would need to get freelancers to do the grading and get paid on actuals. After all, they couldn't have such a large number of permanent employees—the fixed costs would be just too high.

And then there was the issue of checking communication skills. Written communication was relatively easy—the candidate would be asked to write a passage on some topic and this would once again be graded by a freelancer. Verbal communication was a bit tougher, but even this was possible by getting the candidate to record a video on some given topic and upload it. And so on . . .

Now, at this stage, Aman and his co-founders took a very sensible decision. They applied to an accelerator* in Gurgaon and were accepted. Which meant that they were able to get some basic-level funding, as well as mentoring. And, most importantly, they got contacts in companies that could be tapped for recruitment.

With this money, the five young men got down to creating a database of assignments. The idea was to let the candidates work on these assignments, depending on their area of interest. They searched all over the Internet and, wherever necessary, created their own. Now, at this stage, something really interesting happened, so please read carefully. Gradually, a new idea began to take shape

---

* Accelerators are described in detail in Chapter 10. Essentially, they provide you support as well as mentorship to help you scale up your business.

in their collective heads. Why should they restrict themselves only to testing candidates for selection? Why not use these assignments to get them to actually build their skills, so that their chances of selection improved? The more the young men thought about it, the more excited they became. And therefore, even before the launch of Greymeter, the next version was born. They would not only help in shortlisting candidates, but also help them improve their skills by getting them to go through multiple assignments. They also decided on an interesting name for these assignments—they called them 'micro-internships'. After all, if a candidate's résumé were to say that he had worked on several micro-internships, it would sound impressive, wouldn't it?

The next step was to figure out how to reach out to potential freshers. Advertising, even on the Internet, would be frightfully expensive. But our young friends realized that students in colleges—whether in their final year or even earlier—would be far easier and cheaper to reach. All they needed to do was approach the placement cell of each college. And that worked brilliantly. Both the officials as well as the students running this cell were delighted to partner with Greymeter. Anything to help their students get placements. Of course, our founders did not go to A-grade colleges such as the IITs. Instead, they went to the next-level college campuses—both engineering as well as non-engineering. They had rightly figured out that these were the colleges where placement would be an issue and, therefore, students here would be more receptive to the idea.

And then they had another bright idea (this one was over chhola bhatura at a local halwai—it was strange how digestive juices sharpened their thinking faculties, don't you think?). They realized that it was important to get students to register themselves on the Greymeter website. However, it was equally important for them to attempt the micro-internships, so that they could be rated on specific skills, as well as help the candidates improve upon them.

Now, dear reader, we'd like to ask you one question, and the least we expect is an honest answer. What did you focus on during your college days? Was it academics? Come on, be truthful. Or was it girlfriends or boyfriends? Was it music clubs, cricket and generally loitering around in the college cafeteria, chilling? If you happened to be in the latter category, you were probably part of 95 per cent of humanity—the sensible part, of course. Now what would you have done if someone told you they could help you improve your skills to make you more job-ready? Would you immediately dump your guitar and girlfriend, and frantically start working on micro-internships?

Come on. What a silly question. Obviously not. So you can see the problem our young founders faced. They could not get students to work on improving their skills. But they were smart and had a solution ready. They decided to gamify the whole process. A kind of loyalty programme was introduced. Every time a student attempted a micro-internship, he would earn a few 'Grey coins'. If he did well, he would get more Grey coins. And this 'virtual currency' would keep getting accumulated. At any stage, the student could exchange his accumulated Grey coins for goodies such as phone covers or key chains, or if they had earned enough, even things such as footballs and table tennis bats. Great idea, wasn't it? Entice students into doing more and more micro-internships, and get them to win attractive prizes.

One minor detail. What was their revenue model? After all, it was a business, not philanthropy. Simple—charge the companies for each actual recruitment. And for the students it was absolutely free. Similar to the revenue model followed by most placement consultants. In fact, they also tied up with some placement consultants on a fee sharing basis to make their database of students available for potential recruitment.

By now, the excitement had reached fever pitch. The Greymeter website was created and launched with a lot of fanfare. And our young founders started fanning out and visiting colleges. The idea was cool and they were able to partner with ten colleges in and around Delhi alone. In parallel, two of the founders also began to chase companies that planned to recruit freshers. They even started an e-mail campaign where they would send an appropriate mail to the HR department of companies. And the students started pouring in. Gradually, Greymeter built up a sizeable database of around 50,000 students. And looking at this large student base, recruiters started showing interest. Things were definitely looking up.

But of course, they now reached the inevitable roadblock. The funding they had got from the accelerator ran out. And they needed more. Much more. So they approached angel investors . . .

The Pitch and After

The angels around the table were impressed. These young men had latched on to something big. This was a problem waiting to be solved. Many of the investors had themselves wasted huge amounts of time in shortlisting students for recruitment, and they fully appreciated the problem. They also realized that students from second- and third-rung colleges found it extremely difficult to get jobs. This was an idea waiting to explode, and Greymeter could be a market leader in the space.

They also realized a couple of other things. This was a business that had a potentially strong entry barrier. The addition of more and more micro-internships would create a large bank, and any new entrant would need to match it. Further, given the power of social media, the Greymeter brand could actually spread like wildfire among young people.

They were also extremely impressed with Aman, who was the CEO. His enthusiasm was infectious, and he was obviously both passionate and persuasive. Most of all, the angels were impressed with his vision. The only niggling worry was that revenues had barely started coming in. But given the positives, it seemed only a matter of time. And so the investors made up their minds. This was a great opportunity and they were going to fund it. Mentally, they started figuring out which foreign holiday to postpone to raise money . . .

As you can imagine, Greymeter was able to raise a decent amount of funding from the angels, as well as a couple of micro-VC funds—over a crore, in fact. Using this money, they recruited additional people to take care of sales to companies, as well as one person whose job was to add more campuses. They also recruited software developers to enhance their website. And finally, they added a couple of people to create—or search for—more and more micro-internships. Of course, some of the funding was also required for operational expenses such as travel.

Interestingly, their network of campuses grew rapidly and reached a figure of thirty. Consequently, the students in their database also grew to a healthy 1.5 lakh in just over a year. So numbers did not seem to be an issue. There were, however, two issues that the company faced—interesting from our point of view but extremely frustrating from the point of view of the founders. First of all, they realized that the mass recruiters of freshers were mainly the large- and medium-size software companies. And they found—perhaps too late—that these companies wanted bright young people but didn't really care too much about their skill levels. Because they would put these youngsters through four- to six-month-long training programmes, where they would pick up all the skills required for the job. And therefore they were not willing to pay for the candidates they had recruited through Greymeter. In other words, Greymeter was left with the smaller companies that did not have the ability to train people—not as big a market as they had earlier thought. And, of course, scaling up within such a fragmented market was going to be tough.

Secondly, they found that students were quite happy to register on their site but were unwilling to go through the micro-internships—those wonderful micro-internships that our young founders had put together with so much love and affection. And this, in spite of the attractive Grey coins they could earn. Quite naturally, the founders were perplexed. Here were students who were unlikely to get placed at the end of their degrees. All they had to do was try out a few micro-internships, and their chances of getting a job would improve. But no, they wouldn't. Some of them did try out a couple of the micro-internships, but that was it. Not enough to rate them on those skills, and certainly not enough to improve their skill levels. The Greymeter team coaxed and cajoled the students, they sent e-mails that upped the goodies that they could buy with the Grey coins, but the students stubbornly refused to toe the line. As a consequence, there weren't enough students to place, and the expected revenues did not come in. In other words, even within the smaller market they found themselves in, they could not grow.

In life and in business, there are times when you really don't know what's going on. And this was certainly one of them. Till today, the founders are not quite sure what went wrong with their terrific idea. The most plausible explanation was what we have already mentioned earlier in this story. Namely that these students were more keen on enjoying their college life rather than pursuing a career. If this were true, it actually suggested an interesting pivot to the business model. Remember, placement was extremely tough for these students. Now, as students, they probably didn't care, but once they passed out, pressure would build on them. Starting, of course, with their family. '*Ladka kuchh nahin kar raha hai? Abhi tak naukri nahin mili?* (You mean your son is doing nothing? Hasn't he got a job yet?) Tch, tch.' You can, of course, imagine the rest. For girls the problem was likely to be somewhat different. '*Shaadi kara do ji* (Get her married)' is what the aunts were likely to say. And once the pressure built up, the young students— actually ex-students now—would be likely to become more and more desperate for jobs. And this was where Greymeter could be the saviour!

So what should the founders have done? Probably onboarded students when they were students, and kept them engaged with other exciting activities such as games, chats and other interesting titbits. They could have focused on jobs and skills, *only after these students had passed out of college*, when their neighbours' tongues began to wag. That's the time when these youngsters would be more likely to attempt the micro-internships and, therefore, get ready for the job market. Yes, it would not be as huge a business as they had earlier thought, but it could certainly have become a viable one.

However, this also meant that the company needed to survive for some more time without any revenue. Already their funds had come down to rock bottom, and, without revenues, investors were not willing to put in more funds. And so our young friends decided with a heavy heart to shut down the business and distribute whatever meagre funds were left to their existing investors. A sad end to a very promising story!

Shut the company they did, but you can imagine the terrific learning our young friends took away from this experience. It's a good idea to see what Aman has to say on the subject:

One of our biggest learnings has been that we need to understand the thinking of investors—what they are looking for and what their objectives and time frames are. These must align with the business. We realized that most investors look for three things:

a) Are you solving a real problem?
b) Is there a large enough market size?
c) Can you scale up rapidly within this market size and give us an exit?

In our case, we realized that the market size was large but not really huge, because the mass recruiters—typically the large IT companies—were not looking for too many skills in the freshers they took in. Therefore, they were unwilling to pay. Secondly, the students we were targeting were not willing to put in the effort, so even within the smaller recruiter community, we were unable to grow.

To summarize, our venture did not provide either the huge market size or the rapid scaling that our investors wanted. And my sincere advice to anyone building a start-up is, 'Do your market research before you launch, and definitely before you go to your investors.'

Yes, the company did close down, but based on their learning in Greymeter, all the founders are now doing well in their respective fields. For instance, our friend Aman has started a new venture called Fruitish. Essentially a branded chain of outlets for hygienic and healthy drinks—fruit juice, shakes, mocktails and the like. It's very popular—we have been there ourselves and tried out his offerings. It's not a huge business—and therefore he doesn't need investors, at least as of now—but it is profitable. At this point, he has outlets in Noida and Gurgaon, but we're sure he will come to your city some day. We strongly believe that he will make a success of this venture. And as angels, we would be happy to invest in him once again. Wouldn't you?

Analysis

This was the story of a start-up that had many things going for it. There was most certainly a PROBLEM waiting to be solved—and recruiters were likely to pay for it. The SIZE OF THE MARKET was huge—after all, just imagine the number of youngsters entering the job market every year. SCALABILITY was not an issue, since everything was online. The founders definitely had an INNOVATIVE solution to the placement problem. Further, a large bank of micro-internships would provide the much-needed ENTRY BARRIER. And the TEAM was headed by a founder who was pushy, clear-headed and enthusiastic. After all, what more could investors expect from a start-up?

But no—things clearly didn't work out. Simply because students were not willing to put in the effort required to build up or even check out their skills. In hindsight, this was the big RISK in the entire project, but only in hindsight. Initially no one could ever have imagined that students would have this kind of attitude. And where did this show up? In the TRACTION, of course! Or rather, the lack of it. And therefore, in the lack of a proven EARNINGS MODEL. The investors got caught up in the excitement of a great business idea and ignored this extremely important issue. Of course, they also learnt in the process, and are now far more careful. We doubt if they will invest in any start-up without seeing sufficient TRACTION first.

The Impact of the Coronavirus—or Any Other Crisis

Now this is really interesting. You would know that the COVID-19 crisis has had a major negative impact on several industries. And therefore on the number of jobs in these industries. Which means that the number of candidates competing for the same job goes up. And that means . . .

That's right. Candidates need to enhance their skill levels to increase their chances of getting a job. But isn't that exactly what Greymeter was doing? Further, education and training are going increasingly online in today's world. Once again, that's what Greymeter did. In other words, had Greymeter been launched in the post-COVID-19 world, it could potentially have boomed.

Now can you smell an opportunity here? Of course you can. If your start-up is doing anything in the area of skill enhancement or placement, you are in great shape. And if you're doing this online, so much the better. Investors are on the lookout for such start-ups and funding is going to be a lot easier. Remember, my friend, every crisis brings along its share of opportunities. And it's up to you to grab them!

Finally, this is what our PERSISTENT table looks like:

The PERSISTENT Approach Applied to Greymeter

	Issue	Greymeter
P	**PROBLEM:** Are you solving a real problem? Will people pay?	Placement for freshers is a major problem, both for candidates as well as for recruiters.
E	**EARNINGS MODEL**	Revenues in the form of commissions from employers. However, this was not proven, since there was very little TRACTION.
R	**RISKS** and how you will mitigate them	Students unwilling to put in the effort. Large recruiters unwilling to pay.
S	**SIZE OF THE MARKET**	Large, but limited to the smaller recruiters. Therefore highly fragmented.
I	**INNOVATION**	Online, gamified framework for skill building and testing.
S	**SCALABILITY**	Entirely online and therefore scalable.
T	**TEAM**, starting with the founders	Highly enthusiastic founder, passionate about his business, very persuasive.
E	**ENTRY BARRIERS**	Over time, a large bank of micro-internships.
N	**NICHE:** When the market is crowded, identify a niche	-
T	**TRACTION**	Very little.

Let's Meet Deep Kalra, Founder and Executive Chairman, MakeMyTrip

Who hasn't heard of MakeMyTrip? The famous market leader in anything to do with travel—whether it is booking flights, hotels, taxis, buses or just about anything else. And its equally well-known founder and Executive Chairman, Deep Kalra. Deep has successfully built a travel juggernaut and listed it on the prestigious NASDAQ stock exchange. When we requested Deep to share his experiences for the benefit of the readers of this book, he was more than willing. And this is what he had to say:

> To be a successful entrepreneur, you must have a good idea. An idea that solves the customer's pain point and not just something that is nice to have. 'Be an Anacin and not a vitamin for the customer.' However, a good idea is definitely not the end of the story. Please remember, most good ideas are not new. The have probably already occurred to people, and most of them have been converted into businesses. So you've got to figure out how you can do it better than the others. And at scale. And that is what investors look for—a good idea that solves the customer's pain point, does it better than competitors and is able to scale up.

And now the next question—do you really need funding? First of all, if you are developing a product, you definitely need funding, because your revenue will kick in only after the product is ready. If you are in a digital B2C business, you certainly do. Because you need to build your brand quickly, and for that you need money. Very few companies can build such a brand without money. On the other hand, if you are in a B2B business, you may be able to delay the funding, because these businesses depend on good old sales. One caveat—even in a B2B business, you may still require funding to get working capital. Because B2B sales cycles are typically long, and even after you have made the sale, your receivables are likely to be high. But, in any case, try and get funding from your friends and family first—because they will not impose the stringent terms and conditions that external investors will.

Okay, so you've got funding from friends and family, and you've stretched it as far as you could. And now you need to go to external investors. The fundamental issue you must understand is: What do investors look for in an entrepreneur? First of all, conviction in the business is critical. The founder may not give out the magic sauce as yet—after all, he is probably talking to multiple investors and doesn't know who will ultimately come on board. But he himself must carry that conviction. Flexibility is also important—most start-ups will need to pivot several times in their lifetime, and smart entrepreneurs have the ability to pivot.

And now the same question in reverse: What should you as the entrepreneur look for in investors before you take their money? Please remember, who you get the money from is as important—if not more—than the actual money. After all, you don't want the investor to be breathing down your neck all the time asking for an exit, do you? So look for investors for whom this is 'play money'. In other words, money that has been written off, where he is willing to take a risk and doesn't expect quick returns.

So how do you start? Let me give you a suggested process. First of all, write a document about your business. Not a PPT—a detailed document of perhaps six to eight pages. If you can write this, you have a concept. This, by the way, is your teaser—or the trailer of your movie, if you prefer. Get your friends or family to read it. Does it excite them? If it doesn't, you probably need to go back to the drawing board. But if it does, go in for the next step—which is to make an honest plan. I say honest because far too many entrepreneurs make grand plans that even they do not feel they can achieve. Again, share this plan with your family and friends, and try and get them to break it. Once you get through this round, create a longer, more detailed version. Finally, you get down to the actual presentation. Make your PPT, record your talk and play it back. Perhaps share it with friends. You will be surprised at how bad it is the first time. Ask for candid feedback, and keep on modifying it till you are satisfied.

Remember, fundraising is a time-consuming process—and it takes your focus away from growing your business. In the early rounds, you would be going to angels and angel networks. But in the later rounds, when you need to go to VCs, try and go to those where the likelihood of getting money is higher. Or engage an adviser or investment banker. They will do the first level of selling for you, and incidentally they have great contacts. They will also get honest answers from VCs, which you, as the entrepreneur, might not—and that can help you significantly. And finally, they do a great job of 'dressing up the bride'. Let them take their 3 per cent—believe me, it's worth it to get the balance 97 per cent.

One last piece of advice. Building a company demands patience. You will often be in tough, frustrating situations. Remember, it takes at least five–six years to build your company, and maybe ten years for it to become really solid. It is certainly not an overnight affair. So my advice to all would-be entrepreneurs is: *Just hang in there*. Be patient and keep focusing on the business, and you'll be able to live through the ups and downs. Just remember, don't focus on becoming a unicorn—focus on your business. Valuations will happen.

So all the best to all budding entrepreneurs reading this book.

Thanks a lot, Deep. It was great meeting you. And your advice will definitely help our young—and perhaps not-so-young—founders.

6

Purewater: The Brilliant R&D Project

The Pitch

The city was Bengaluru, and the atmosphere around the table electric. Faces flushed with excitement, the hardened angels stared at the founders of Purewater in awe. After all those so-so start-ups they had been listening to, this was the real thing. They almost jumped over each other . . .

But hang on. We're getting carried away. Let's look at the business, or rather, the product, for that is what it was. It was a product designed by two young engineers. And it could purify ordinary tap water and make it safe for drinking.

Aha! Now you're getting the picture. But here's the killer: This product was substantially cheaper than any of the other, more established products in the market. And could, therefore, be installed even in lower-income households. Not just in cities, but in villages too. Just imagine—finally someone had developed a cost-effective solution for creating safe, potable water. Could India possibly ask for anything more?

So you get the idea. And you begin to realize why the angels around the table were so excited. The engineers among the angels quizzed and questioned the young founders repeatedly, and were quite satisfied with the solution. At the moment the company was in pilot mode and manufacturing would ultimately be outsourced. That made sense—after all, the key was the design. The team had even applied for a patent.

Of course, there was the issue of generating sales, but the founders clearly said they would appoint distributors. Which made eminent sense, since they were planning to go pan-India on a massive scale. So a couple of deal leads were appointed—these were members across the table who were willing to study the project and its viability in more detail.

The deal leads spent time with these youngsters, studied the business model in detail and came back quite satisfied. 'This is a gold mine,' they said with a quiet smile. 'With drinking water being such a massive issue in our country, these guys cannot go wrong. And they have a good, workable design. However, what is most important is that they hit the ground running and establish themselves quickly in the market. That's the only way to keep out copycats.' And so the youngsters were called back for one final discussion. But this was felt to be a formality and most people in the angel network were simply itching to get their hands on their chequebooks.

Now, as the young founders trooped into the room for the meeting, a keen observer would have noticed that they were, if anything, even more excited than they were during the first meeting. And the reason soon came out. 'We are now working on our next product. This one will be a lightweight, portable water purifier—so you can actually carry it with you when going out of town. No more expensive bottled water when you are travelling,' they blurted out. And they were grinning from ear to ear, just waiting for the applause.

There was stunned silence in the room. 'What about the existing product?'

'Yes, of course that's still there. But this will be the real thing—just imagine what it can do for travellers.'

'What about the distributors you were to appoint?'

'Yes, we do plan to appoint them once we have the portable product out. That's just a matter of a few months.'

'A few months?' one of the angels exploded. 'You mean you still haven't done it?'

'No, but that's easy. It will be done.'

The battle-scarred angels looked at each other. Slowly they let out their collective breaths. Chequebooks and pens went back into their jacket pockets—figuratively, of course. It was such a pity. Great product, huge market, phenomenal timing, but . . .

One of the angels put it succinctly. 'Boss, these guys have turned it into an R&D project.'

The angels nodded and quietly said goodbye to the millions they had been planning to make. And the Jaguars they might have bought. And the youngsters went back to work on their R&D project. No funding for them.

Analysis

Dear reader, you probably don't need to read this analysis. You must have figured out what went wrong with this potentially wonderful story. That's right—if you examine our PERSISTENT model, this project ticked perhaps all the right boxes. Huge PROBLEM waiting to be solved, massive SIZE OF THE MARKET, no problem with SCALABILITY—they could easily tie up with a low-cost manufacturer—very INNOVATIVE solution, etc.

All the boxes but one. Perhaps the most critical one. Namely the TEAM. These guys were good techies but they had no business sense. They had fallen in love with their own product and their purpose seemed to be to create newer and newer products, rather than taking them to market and scaling up the business. And, by the way, this is a very common phenomenon with techie-driven start-ups.

What's the solution? Simple. *One of the founders must have a business orientation.* If not, the founders need to rope in someone at the CEO level who understands and can drive business. In our experience, far too many promising start-ups have died an early, unnatural death simply because it was driven by techies with no clue about business.

Don't get us wrong. We are not saying techies cannot build great businesses. Many terrific businesses have been built by engineers, computer scientists and the like. But someone with business sense needs to understand and drive the business—that's all!

The Impact of the Coronavirus—or Any Other Crisis

Purewater is the kind of business that everyone dreams of starting. Simply because it is immune to any crisis. Whether it is the coronavirus or the dot-com bust of 2001 or the global financial crisis of 2008, this kind of business cannot and will not be impacted. Yes, there may be a temporary delay in funding, but ultimately you'll get your money.

The simple message, therefore, is this: Look for businesses that are crisis-proof. And you'll get your money sooner or later.

Finally, let's look at the PERSISTENT approach as applied to Purewater:

The PERSISTENT Approach Applied to Purewater

	Issue	Purewater
P	**PROBLEM:** Are you solving a real problem? Will people pay?	Solution for making ordinary tap water drinkable.
E	**EARNINGS MODEL**	Revenue from products sales. Unit economics positive.
R	**RISKS** and how you will mitigate them	Someone copying the product.
S	**SIZE OF THE MARKET**	Massive.
I	**INNOVATION**	Innovative design.
S	**SCALABILITY**	Product with no manual intervention and, therefore, highly scalable.
T	**TEAM**, starting with the founders	Pure tech people, with no business sense.
E	**ENTRY BARRIERS**	Low-cost, patented solution. Over time, the brand.
N	**NICHE:** When the market is crowded, identify a niche	-
T	**TRACTION**	In pilot mode at the time of applying for funding.

7

No Money for Wedding Gifts

The young couple had just got back from their honeymoon. Excited as ever, they were sitting in their living room, steaming cups of tea in their hands and opening the vast array of wedding gifts around them.

'One more crockery set,' she said. 'That makes four.'

'Here's a fifth one,' he chipped in. 'And by the way, this large package looks like another one.'

The two looked at each other. 'What will we do with six crockery sets? Anyway Mom has given us two. And what about the five Borosil carafes and four pressure cookers? What are we going to do with all of this?'

Sounds familiar? Of course it does. Because that's invariably what happens with wedding gifts. Every guest wants to gift something that the young couple starting their life together will find useful. And what could be more useful than a crockery set?

But *six* crockery sets? What could be more useless?

And that, dear reader, is precisely the problem Cyrus Shaadikaranewala planned to solve. Cyrus had just been to the US to attend the wedding of his cousin, and had been extremely impressed with the concept of wedding-gift registries.

You see, in several Western countries, when a young couple decides to get married, they sit down and make a list of all the things they would like to get as gifts. That's right—it's the couple that decides this, not the guests at the wedding. This could include mundane things such as cutlery and crockery sets, or even exquisite gifts such as a Mediterranean cruise. It's another issue that this often leads to the first major disagreement between the two lovebirds— after all, they are not likely to agree on all gifts, are they? Assuming the wedding does not fall through as a consequence, the next step is to put up this list on a wedding-gift registry. These are websites that are designed specially for this purpose—they permit couples to put up their wish lists on the site.

How do guests access this list? Simple. The wedding card contains the URL of the registry. In fact, if it's an e-card, things are even simpler, because a link to the registry is then inserted into the card. The rest is obvious. Guests who receive the card follow the link to reach the registry, and thereby get access to the wish list of the young couple. Each guest can then pick and choose what he or she would like to gift the couple, and pay for it. This gift is then attractively wrapped by the registry and delivered to the couple, say, a week after the wedding.

There is more. Sometimes a gift is expensive and the registry permits multiple guests to share the cost. A pragmatic way to ensure that couples actually get what they want rather than being saddled with multiple crockery sets.

And that, ladies and gentlemen, is precisely the kind of wedding-gift registry that Cyrus wanted to set up in India. The concept was new. Some people were trying it out, but it was still early days. Cyrus believed he could be a market leader in the space. And so he went about planning his venture, which we will call Wedgift.com, as the real name has been masked. First of all, while a young couple might put up their wish list on Wedgift, he needed to find out which kinds of guests would use it. And so he spoke to several friends. The unanimous opinion was that this would only work with youngsters, typically friends of the couple getting married. Most older people were likely to continue with the age-old tradition of giving cash, and were unlikely to use Wedgift. Which was fine. Even if usage was restricted to only friends, the market size would still potentially be very large.

The next step, of course, was to identify possible gift items that they could list on their website which guests could choose from. Interestingly, they also had the option of gift vouchers, which would give the couple flexibility to choose their gifts after the marriage. All these were then made available on the website. Importantly, only the guests were asked to pay for their gifts. The couple did not have to pay anything for putting up their wish list.

Then there was the job of identifying vendors for all these items and negotiating with them. There was an interesting option of tying up with a company such as Flipkart (or Amazon), where Wedgift would operate and manage the gift registry and Flipkart would source the gifts from their vendors and deliver them. However, this option was dumped for a very simple reason. You see, the nature of the gifts and the occasion necessitated great packaging—gift-wrapping along with perhaps a ribbon and a card. It was unlikely that Flipkart would take care of this for a much smaller, niche business. Further, the wrapping could get damaged, the card and the ribbon could get crushed during delivery, and so on. In other words, they needed specialized packaging and delivery, which regular e-commerce vendors were not likely to provide. Specialized vendors were required, and after negotiations these vendors were finalized.

And finally, there was the big daddy of them all—marketing. Here Cyrus did something really smart. He realized that a typical Indian wedding uses multiple service providers—banquet halls, caterers, photographers, wedding-card designers and, of course, in some cases, wedding planners themselves. He spoke to several of these providers and worked out a barter arrangement, where they would pass on their clients to him and, in turn, he would pass on his own clients to them. Effectively free marketing. Smart, wasn't it?

In addition, he was able to get press coverage for his company by using contacts of his friends, which was once again free.

Now that everything was in place, Cyrus needed customers. Fortunately, he was able to get two couples—friends of friends—to create their wish list on the Wedgift registry. And he was now all set to go to the next step. The big, big step where he would ask angel investors to put their hard-earned money into his venture.

The Pitch

The angels gathered in the room were definitely interested. This was a concept that was new to India, but very popular in the Western world. And given the huge popularity of Western movies and serials in India, as well as increased travel to the US and Europe, such a concept was bound to catch on. At least among the younger generation. Admittedly, the older generation would continue to give cash in most cases, but friends of the couple, in other words the younger generation, formed a huge target segment. There was also the benefit of an 'early mover advantage'. Being among the first to get into this space, Wedgift had a great chance to become a market leader, provided they got their act right.

There was also the benefit of marketing through their partners. Assuming wedding planners, photographers and card designers were okay promoting the company on a reciprocal basis, marketing costs were virtually nil. Plus this was a brilliant case for word-of-mouth-based promotion. Once a couple went through this process, assuming both they and their friends had had a pleasant experience, all their unmarried friends would automatically become potential customers for Wedgift when they got married. Of course, if they got divorced and remarried, so much the better—at least for Wedgift.

Fortunately, Cyrus was also extremely knowledgeable about the business. And passionate as well. All questions the angels fired at him were answered satisfactorily and in great detail. In other words, things seemed to be going just fine.

However, there was the flip side as well. First of all, there was the cultural issue. In India, while it was perfectly all right to expect a wedding gift, you could not demand one. One of the angels mimicked a typical response from a mother to her daughter who was about to get married, '*Hai hai, tu gift mangegi? Ki ho gaya hai tenu? Naak katwayegi saaddi* [You mean, you'll actually ask people for gifts? How embarrassing]?' (Incidentally, this snippet is in Punjabi, one of the most colourful and expressive languages known to mankind.) Indians are known for their deep-rooted cultural values. Would they be willing to change? Even if the gift registry were only circulated to friends, would the parents of the young couple allow them to do so, with the possibility of ridicule staring them in the face?

And then one of the angels had a bright idea. 'How do your prices compare with those on Amazon?'

'They are obviously higher, since we do not have their volumes, and therefore cannot get huge discounts.'

'So what's to prevent a guest checking the couple's wish list on the Wedgift site, and then buying the gift on Amazon?' This statement was made with a touch of pride, as if to say, 'So there.'

For the first time Cyrus sounded a bit uncertain. 'Yes, that could happen. But some of our products are services such as cruises and stays in resorts, which you will not get on Amazon. Also, products are gift-wrapped, saving the guest a lot of hassle.' There was an attempt to be confident, but the keen observer would have made out a slight hesitation.

The angels looked at each other. Perhaps the business was not as great as they had earlier thought. And then, of course, there was the possibility of Amazon or Flipkart identifying it as a niche and getting into it themselves. Building in a wish list into the software was no big deal, and the only thing to add was the gift-wrapping. Not really an issue if they decided to get in. Hmmm . . . Maybe . . .

And so the meeting ended on a somewhat sombre note. What had initially appeared to be a great idea was perhaps not so great, after all. Too many uncertainties and no real entry barrier. The angels quietly put away their chequebooks—figuratively, of course—and trooped out of the room to pick up their cups of coffee. Investments could wait.

Analysis

What happened in the case of Wedgift is fairly evident, isn't it? There was definitely a PROBLEM waiting to be solved. It made eminent sense to get guests to give the couple gifts that they really wanted. Even though there was a cultural issue and the concept had not yet been tried out in India, it seemed workable, at least among friends. In other words, a great NICHE within the e-commerce space—and a large enough one. And it was undoubtedly an INNOVATIVE solution—tried and tested internationally. If the concept caught on, the SIZE OF THE MARKET was immense, given the propensity of young people in India to use the Internet. It was also highly SCALABLE, since the only real manual intervention was the packaging and delivery—which could also be outsourced over time. In fact, the concept could easily go viral. Above all, the TEAM—in this case a one-man show—was extremely impressive—passionate and knowledgeable.

But the major, major issue was the RISK. What if a guest were to check out the wish list on their website and then buy the same gift from Amazon or Flipkart? So much cheaper. And, of course, the possibility of Amazon and Flipkart entering the same business. There was no real ENTRY BARRIER in this business—especially for these giants who only needed minor tweaking to enter the gift-registry business. No sir. It simply didn't make sense.

And therefore the angels, in their wisdom, said, 'No, thank you!'

The Impact of the Coronavirus—or Any Other Crisis

We're sure you know the answer by now. Many people are likely to cut down on shopping at physical outlets such as malls and move to online purchasing. Therefore, a business such as Wedgift, which is entirely online, is likely to benefit. Of course, the other problems such as people checking out a gift on Wedgift and then buying it on Amazon remains. But the message remains the same—online is a good way to go!

Finally, we summarize this analysis as usual, in our PERSISTENT table:

The PERSISTENT Approach Applied to Wedgift

	Issue	Wedgift
P	**PROBLEM:** Are you solving a real problem? Will people pay?	The problem of unwanted wedding gifts. People would obviously pay to buy these gifts.
E	**EARNINGS MODEL**	Margin earned on each gift purchased.
R	**RISKS** and how you will mitigate them	People checking the wish list on Wedgift.com and then buying their gift at much lower rates on Amazon or Flipkart.
S	**SIZE OF THE MARKET**	Large, but unproven.
I	**INNOVATION**	Innovative solution, not yet tried out in India.
S	**SCALABILITY**	Scalable. The manual intervention was limited to packaging and delivery, which could easily be outsourced.
T	**TEAM**, starting with the founders	Highly knowledgeable and passionate founder.
E	**ENTRY BARRIERS**	Very low, especially for e-commerce companies that are already into online sales.
N	**NICHE:** When the market is crowded, identify a niche	A clear and large niche in the e-commerce space.
T	**TRACTION**	Two registries at the time of making the pitch.

8

Plenty of Fashionchat but No Funding

Bobby P. was very keen on buying a new dress. But she desperately wanted the opinion of her friends. After all, buying a dress was a group activity. Her friend Kavita was a good person to check with—she was a conservative dresser, and what she approved would probably pass muster with Bobby's parents. On the other hand, there was Jinx, who was super-fashionable and possessed great personal style. She had to be involved. And, of course, Salma—her best friend from school. And Geeta. And Preeti. And Mohini. And, oh, how could she possibly forget her boyfriend Sammy (short for Samvardhananand—why anyone would shorten such a nice, simple name such as Samvardhananand to Sammy, we don't know).

Now, as the astute reader would have observed, there was a teeny weeny problem. She couldn't possibly take all these people along with her when she went shopping. Some were preparing for their exams. Sammy was out of town. Kavita and Preeti were attending a wedding . . .

So Bobby was left to her own devices. And that set her thinking. In today's day and age, why couldn't this be done online? Why couldn't she visit a showroom, invite her friends to a chat session and share photographs of the dresses available there? Or even photographs of Bobby herself wearing those dresses? And get feedback from her friends on the spot? In fact, it could even set off an interesting debate between the conservative Kavita and the highly innovative Jinx.

A spark of an idea had been kindled, and Bobby was excited. Why not launch such a site? A kind of Facebook, specifically for fashion? As she warmed to the theme, she decided to go to her favourite café and treat herself to a chocolate fantasy. (For the uninitiated reader, a chocolate fantasy is a delightful pastry overflowing with an almost sinful amount of yummy, molten chocolate. As you might imagine, it was one of Bobby's many favourites. She claimed it helped her think.)

And so, in between mouthfuls of chocolate fantasy, the idea began to take shape. Why not have links from the site to fashion brands as well as outlets? So buyers could actually browse the site and discuss what was available in the market with their friends, even before going to the outlet? And then the site could point them to the nearest outlet that sold these dresses. She could also get in experts who would answer questions on different kinds of fabrics. In fact, it could extend to handbags and belts and shoes and . . .

In short, a one-stop portal for anything to do with fashion. It was so exciting! Fashion was so close to Bobby's heart. This was a whole new world waiting to be created. Charged up by now, Bobby decided to name her venture Fashionchat (name changed). Yes, over her second chocolate fantasy, even the name had been decided. Bobby was a quick decision maker, you see.

So Bobby launched Fashionchat.com. To get fashion lovers together for what she called 'group shopping'. Fortunately, she had worked in a multinational for six years and had therefore saved up some money. This, along with some funds provided by her parents, formed the initial capital for the venture. With this she put together a team to develop the site. And then, of course, there was the marketing—which was predominantly Google AdWords and some amount of SEO—search engine optimization for the uninitiated reader.

Things moved slowly but surely. Bobby managed to get several thousand registrations on her site. Unfortunately, by then, the money ran out and she needed funds. For two reasons. First of all, content on the site had to be expanded and updated on a daily basis—after all, she was dealing with the highly volatile area of fashion. And secondly, this was a new concept and required significant marketing spend to rope in a large audience.

The long and short of it was that she needed money. And who better than angel investors to approach?

The Pitch

The hard-nosed angels seated around the table listened intently to Bobby. And they couldn't help being swayed by her enthusiasm. They realized that this was something different—perhaps something that hadn't been tried out in the country before. The potential was clearly huge and, given the rising consumerism in India, this was the right time to launch it. Further, Bobby had done her homework well and had her facts on her fingertips, which the angels clearly appreciated.

'How do you plan to increase your registrations? You'll need to go far, far beyond just a few thousand,' asked one of the angels.

'We plan to spend heavily on both online marketing—essentially Google AdWords—and SEO. And we expect the concept to go viral in the age group we are targeting.'

That made sense, and the angels nodded. However, there was still one potentially explosive question left. 'What's your revenue model?'

'At this point, we do not have any revenue. Even for the foreseeable future we have not planned for any revenue. Our focus is to build a large community with a common interest in fashion.'

'But at some stage you would need to generate revenue. Is this going to be advertisement-based?'

'Well, yes, we do plan to monetize our venture through ads. But that's in the future. We haven't really thought of revenues yet.'

'If you are looking at ad-based revenues, you'll need a much, much larger community. And that will require both time and lots of funding. Perhaps multiple rounds. With no sight of revenues,' said one of the angels, and he looked around meaningfully at the others. As if on cue, most of the angels nodded. They wanted to see revenues. Without revenues, they were not really willing to invest in the venture. And this seemed to be a long gestation project.

'Why don't you sell garments and accessories online? You'll at least have revenue to support the build-up of your community,' said another angel.

'We thought of that,' replied Bobby, 'but we would like to maintain a neutral image. Selling on our site would kill that image and therefore kill the chances of building our community.' Bobby seemed confident as she said this, but she had begun to realize that all was not well. She desperately needed a chocolate fantasy to pep her up again. Because the angels were obviously not happy. All except one, who kept repeating, 'Guys, this is like a specialized version of Facebook. When Facebook started, it had no revenue. The initial years were simply focused on building its huge community. And look at it now. Admittedly it will take time, but I believe it is worth investing in.'

Unfortunately, this was a lone voice, and at the end of the presentation, a crestfallen Bobby realized that the deal had been dropped. A great idea, perhaps, but with no revenue in sight, there were no takers.

Analysis

The case of Fashionchat is somewhat unique. Let's start by analysing it within our PERSISTENT framework.

Undoubtedly there was a PROBLEM—or, rather, an opportunity. That of getting young people to shop along with their friends—even though they might not be physically present. When combined with expert advice on the subject, it was a powerful social media tool—something that did not exist at the time the presentation was made. However, if you look closely at our PERSISTENT model, it is not enough to solve a problem or tap into an opportunity. *People have to be willing to pay for it.* And that was precisely the problem. In today's day and age, no one pays for WhatsApp or Facebook. No one pays for searching the web through Google. In fact, no one pays for Gmail or Hotmail or any of the other commonly available mail services. Most of these highly successful businesses get their revenue through other means such as advertising. So why would anyone pay to use Fashionchat? No sir, revenues would need to come in through ads, in much the same manner as Google or Facebook.

However—and this is a HUGE however—advertisers on portals such as Facebook are willing to pay because of the very large community that Facebook has managed to build. By implication, they might be willing to pay for ads on Fashionchat, but only if its community were large enough. Obviously not as large as Facebook, but still large enough in the Indian context. And that, ladies and gentlemen, was the problem. Bobby needed hefty amounts of funding to build such a large community before she started getting revenues. And the angels wanted to see revenues reasonably early, before they parted with their money. Even if they did, the amounts would usually not be enough for Fashionchat to build the huge user base it needed to. A typical chicken-and-egg situation, sadly.

Now here's the twist in the story. Did you notice that one angel sitting in the corner of the room who was convinced? And was trying to convince the others in the room? That's right—we knew you'd notice him. It was even likely that he would have invested a few lakhs in Bobby's venture. Unfortunately, those few lakhs wouldn't have been enough to help Bobby, which is why the entire deal was called off.

What was so different about this one particular angel? Remember, all investors are not alike. There are some who have a time horizon of three or four years, and would like to get returns on their investments within this period. These investors look at revenues. On the other hand, there are those who recognize a great long-term opportunity and are willing to wait for revenues. The problem, of course, is that the former greatly outnumber the latter. Fortunately, however, investors of the second kind do exist. Many of these are the HNI angels—those who invest not Rs 3–5 lakh but perhaps Rs 50 lakh, Rs 1 crore or even more. Obviously they are finicky. They would analyse the business in terrific detail before putting in their money. But when they do decide to part with their money, it is usually large sums.

And therefore the solution to Bobby's problem emerges. Identify those few wealthy angels who are willing to take a long-term bet. You might need just three or four such investors—maybe even fewer. These are the investors who will not ask for quick revenues but would be willing to wait patiently for the community to build up. The kind of investors who would have invested in Facebook or Google or even Hotmail, when these ventures were launched. After all, that's why these investors are wealthy, in the first place!

By the way, it is interesting to compare Fashionchat with SQRRL from Chapter 4. SQRRL was in a very similar situation, where it had no immediate revenues and needed large amounts of funding to grow. The difference, of course, is that SQRRL did have a revenue model—but one that would be implemented in future. It would charge for transactions such as the purchase of insurance products. It's only that it had delayed charging till its customers were hooked. Fashionchat, on the other hand, did not have a revenue model at all. And therefore SQRRL was able to raise funding, whereas Fashionchat simply could not.

And that's a good note on which to end this story. In case you are in a B2C business without any immediate revenues, you will definitely need large funding. You may be able to get this kind of funding from angels, but it is more likely that you'll need to go to the larger ones, or even to VC funds. Of course, the caveat is that you should have put in a large amount yourself—which the founders of SQRRL had. Why else would anyone else invest?

Of course, you must remember that, often, this is also a matter of luck. Perhaps Bobby had made her pitch to the angels soon after some other investments had bombed and the angels were licking their wounds. Or after a major stock market crash. Please remember, getting funding is not based on a formula. You have guidelines, but they are, after all, guidelines. They will work in many cases, but there will be those where they may not. And that's also true of much of life, isn't it?

Finally, here's our PERSISTENT table:

The PERSISTENT Approach Applied to Fashionchat

	Issue	Fashionchat
P	PROBLEM: Are you solving a real problem? Will people pay?	Yes, but people would not pay for it. Therefore the revenue model was not clear.
E	EARNINGS MODEL	Not yet planned for.
R	RISKS and how you will mitigate them	If the opportunity was large enough, Facebook could enter the business.
S	SIZE OF THE MARKET	Very large.
I	INNOVATION	Social media focused on fashion.
S	SCALABILITY	Very high. Large market, with no manual intervention.
T	TEAM, starting with the founders	Entrepreneur focused and passionate about her project.
E	ENTRY BARRIERS	Initially none. Over time—a large community as well as a large pool of experts and other partners.
N	NICHE: When the market is crowded, identify a niche	Social media focused on fashion.
T	TRACTION	A few thousand users.

9

Toppernotes for Non-Toppers

It was that dreaded time of the year once again. Just two weeks to go for the final Class IX exams. And as usual, Chhotu was completely unprepared. After all, with the cricket series against Australia and all those terrific new movies in town, how could anyone be expected to do something as stupid as studying? 'If only I could get Maggu's notes. He is our class topper and makes excellent notes in class. With those notes, I would just sail through the exams,' he said one evening to his older cousin Aditi.

The discussion then turned towards the inevitable cricket and the heated debate around Dhoni's potential retirement. But Aditi wasn't really listening. That one statement of Chhotu's remained stuck in her mind, 'If only I could get Maggu's notes . . .'

'Why not?' Aditi kept thinking. 'Why can't my cousin get Maggu's notes? Or Amit's notes or Shankar's notes, or notes from any other good student in class? In fact, why can't he get notes from any other good student anywhere in the country? Why does the student have to be from his class?'

The more she thought about it, the more excited Aditi became. So much so that she actually forgot about her evening date with her boyfriend—with fairly disastrous consequences. However, Aditi's love life is not really what we want to discuss here, so let's focus on what she had been thinking about. Aditi's mind was whirring with a terrific business concept. Students across the country needed good notes to study from. And good notes were not easy to come by, simply because many good students were unwilling to share them. Why not build a business around notes? Have a huge database of class notes picked up from good students—for a fee, naturally. Several good students would relish the prospect of additional pocket money and perhaps be willing to upload their notes. And all those students who spent their time in far more useful pursuits, such as making paper rockets or doodling in class, would have access to these notes. Once again for a fee. Taking the idea a step forward, Aditi could actually give some kind of royalty to those students who had uploaded their notes, based on usage. What a great idea!

Aditi was so excited that she even forgot to take a bath (the reader should note that this was summertime in Delhi). She rushed over and discussed the idea with a couple of friends. Fortunately, they were equally excited and agreed to join her in this venture. And so, with a lot of fanfare, Toppernotes was born.

There were, of course, some issues to be ironed out. The quality of the notes being uploaded was critical. They would probably get a lot of useless stuff from average students who only wanted to make money. Aditi and gang had two options to take care of this. One was to have a team of teachers who would check everything before it was uploaded. However, this was likely to be expensive, because they would probably have a huge number of notes and couldn't possibly pay to have them all checked. Further, the teachers would probably veto most of the material and instead attempt to put up their own notes—and, once again, this would be an expensive option. And so this option was knocked out. What they finally decided on was a user-rating system—rather like the one used by Tripadvisor and Ola Cabs—where students who accessed any material would rate the notes they had tried out and the consolidated rating would be available to all new students.

There was, of course, one ticklish issue. Would good students be willing to share their notes? Or would they feel they were competing with other students and therefore refuse to share them, even for a bit of extra pocket money? At least in the senior classes, closer to their board exams, this could be the case. However, the founders were not too worried about this. Students could always upload their notes from the previous year—after all, this would only go to juniors, and they were not in competition with juniors. At least the good students were not.

So our young founders started off their brand-new venture by developing the portal where students would upload their notes and other students would download them. However, very soon they came up against a familiar problem. They needed more money. For constantly developing and upgrading the site, for paying students to upload their content and, above all, for marketing.

Therefore they did what all other founders in their position would have done—they approached a set of angel investors.

The Pitch

The angels around the table listened carefully to Aditi and her co-founders. It seemed like a good idea. Evidently, most of the angels had played, sung and danced their way through school, with academics being a most unnecessary evil. They understood exactly what Chhotu had been going through. Incidentally, by the usual twist of fate, many of them were now parents and facing exactly the same problem with their own kids. So they realized that the problem undoubtedly existed, and these youngsters did have a solution. But like all angels, they still had doubts.

Most importantly, would any student actually pay to download notes? Wouldn't they rather try and get notes from some bright classmate? Yes, some of these classmates might not be willing to share their notes, but there were lots of good as well as kind students in class—surely one or two of them would?

Then there was the issue of rating the notes. It was okay to ask a person who had stayed in a hotel to rate his stay, but would this work for notes? After all, no student has the time when exams are approaching. Everyone is busy cramming. At this stage, a student would only go in for proven notes—definitely not those they were not sure about. Further, a below-average student would not even know whether the notes put up were correct, so how could he be expected to rate them? The student putting up notes could also get his friends to give him a superlative rating. No sir, the angels were not convinced—rating was definitely an issue.

There was also the problem of protecting the material downloaded. It would be so easy for one student to download the notes and then share it with his or her classmates—perhaps he or she might even be able to make money out of this deal! And making the notes available only online, without the option of downloading, was certainly not viable. What if there was no Internet connection at the time a student wanted to study? No, no, that would never do.

The angels were actually caught in no-man's land. Good idea, huge market, highly scalable but too many question marks. And there was no significant traction so far. So they did what sensible angels do—they decided against the deal for the moment. 'Let's give these people some more time and see if the business actually builds up. Till then, we'll stay away,' was the general refrain. And anyway, there were so, so many opportunities coming up every day.

Analysis

This was one of those tantalizing projects that could have gone either way. Great concept, major PROBLEM waiting to be solved, large MARKET SIZE, SCALABLE business, etc. But at the end of the day, there were too many RISKS. The RISK of students not willing to pay for their notes. The RISK of the quality of the notes not being up to the mark—with no real way to tackle the problem. And, of course, the RISK of leakage—of students downloading the material and sharing it with all their classmates.

Interestingly, the angels had not said no. They had only said no for the moment. In case the founders were able to get the business to grow and show decent traction, well, they could always come back. And the angels would be willing to listen to them.

And that, dear reader, is an important bit of learning. Often, investors will have doubts and questions. They might not be willing to invest immediately. And the only way to remove these doubts is to show proof. Namely TRACTION. Show the numbers going up, and you may be able to worm your way into their wallets after some time.

Of course, for this you need money. So what do you do? Cut costs dramatically. Maybe scale down your plans. Don't look for rapid growth—that would anyway need funding. Look for growth that you can manage with the funds you already have. Approach your long-lost chacha or mama—the one with pots of money, who you never really liked. Talk to him nicely, maybe run a few errands for him or clean his car. Who knows . . . ?

Turn the page for our PERSISTENT table:

The PERSISTENT Approach Applied to Toppernotes

	Issue	Toppernotes
P	**PROBLEM:** Are you solving a real problem? Will people pay?	Genuine problem, but would students pay?
E	**EARNINGS MODEL**	Revenue per download.
R	**RISKS** and how you will mitigate them	Students could download the material and then share it, thereby bypassing the site. And the whole issue of the quality of uploaded notes was an open question.
S	**SIZE OF THE MARKET**	Very large.
I	**INNOVATION**	The attempt to convert a local sharing phenomenon into an organized business.
S	**SCALABILITY**	High.
T	**TEAM**, starting with the founders	-
E	**ENTRY BARRIERS**	Possibly high, once they had built up a large bank of notes, as well as a brand.
N	**NICHE:** When the market is crowded, identify a niche	-
T	**TRACTION**	Very little.

Let's Meet Yashish Dahiya, Co-Founder and CEO, PolicyBazaar, PaisaBazaar*

Who hasn't heard of market leaders Policybazaar.com and Paisabazaar.com? And the highly energetic founder and CEO of both, Yashish Dahiya? Of course you have. We're sure you are thinking, quite rightly, that he's a very busy person. But are you aware that this highly successful IIT Delhi and IIMA graduate is a marathon runner? And a national swimming champion at the master's level? No? Even we didn't, till we met him.

This busy, accomplished national champion was kind enough to take time out for us and share his learning over the past several years as an entrepreneur. Just for you readers. So let's see what he had to say:

> There was a time in India when the investment climate had not yet matured, and investors would look for profits early on in the life of a start-up. Which was actually a problem, because many start-ups—particularly those in the B2C space—need

---

* Taken from the authors' personal interview with Yashish Dahiya in 2019.

time to check out the concept, establish a presence and build their brand. Fortunately, the investment environment has matured over the years. And investors have realized that there are multiple stages in a business—starting with the concept, going on to significant revenues and finally leading to profits. They have realized that you cannot artificially speed up this process, and are willing to wait, and give you time to learn. Interestingly, while they are willing to wait for profits, many of them are not willing to wait too long for an exit. So investing has also become a kind of relay race, where one investor invests for a certain period, gets an exit and passes on the baton to the next investor.

However, there is a negative side to this. Unfortunately, entrepreneurs have also changed over the past several years. Earlier, the aim used to be to build a solid business over the years. Now many founders build to exit—in other words, they build to sell. Please remember, an exit cannot be your strategy. It cannot be part of your business plan. For instance, you cannot say, 'I'll prove the concept, and then exit. Let someone else take over.' No boss—you need to deliver. You, as the entrepreneur, are like the pilot of a plane. And you are responsible not only for a safe take-off but also a safe landing at the destination. And for this you must have a long-term plan, where you plan to make profits—perhaps not in the immediate future but definitely at some stage. And your plan cannot be your own exit from the company. Unfortunately, many founders do not follow this principle, and this is one of the prime reasons for failure.

There is another thing that you must remember—don't lie. Never fool the investor, and please don't get into financial jugglery. Remember, investors are smart people, and at some stage you'll be found out. The other issue is that when you lie to investors, you start believing the lie yourself—and that's a real disaster. As an entrepreneur, you have to be honest with yourself, and with your investors. Giving returns to your investor is your responsibility. And remember, he's on your side.

One final word. Creating a business is a long, long process. Just to build an effective moat—or entry barrier—you'll perhaps take ten years. You certainly cannot do it in two years and exit. Therefore patience is the name of the game.

So happy entrepreneurship, and all the best!

That was great advice, Yashish. Thanks a lot. And next time, we'll take advice from you on running marathons!

10

What about Non-Equity Funding?

So far we've seen how different start-ups have raised money through equity. In other words, by getting investors to buy shares in the company. And, of course, we have also seen those who couldn't. But is that the only way to raise money? Surely there are more? Of course there are. So read on . . .

Debt or Loan Funding

Obviously you know what a loan is. It's also called debt funding, where you borrow money at a certain rate of interest. Importantly, you do not give any equity to the lender, and therefore your stake in your start-up is not diluted. So you've got the money, and there's no issue of shares.

Sounds good, doesn't it? But as you are aware, you never get something for nothing. Let's say a bank gives you a loan. Please remember, it is not a donation to a poor entrepreneur—although it often feels like that. It's a loan. And, therefore, it must be paid back. So before giving the loan, the bank must be reasonably certain that they'll get their money back. How do they do this? One simple way is by taking collateral—so if you buy a car through a bank loan, the car will be mortgaged to the bank until the entire money is paid back. Another method is by getting a personal guarantee—which works well where the founder has a rich (and benevolent) father. Failing that, what collateral can a start-up possibly have? Other than perhaps the founder's clothes and watch—and we sincerely hope it doesn't come to that.

So collateral is out for most start-ups. What's the other option? Well, if you've shown profits, or even better, several years of profit, the bank might be convinced and give you a loan. But how many start-ups are profitable, at least in their early days? Isn't the whole purpose of getting funds is to grow and become profitable? So that's out as well. The only option left, therefore, is for the bank to take a personal guarantee. Perhaps from someone known to the founder, who has a proven source of income. If you can get this, that's great. But what if you can't? Does that mean you can't get a loan at all?

No sir. In their keenness to promote start-ups, the Government of India as well as some state governments have rolled out schemes to provide loans without any collateral or personal guarantee. For instance, we have the CGTMSE scheme, or the Credit Guarantee Fund Trust for Micro and Small Enterprises,[*] under which loans are available from several public-sector banks. What does the scheme do? Very simple— if the start-up fails to pay back the loan, the bank can recover the money from the scheme. It is open to companies whose founders have professional qualifications and are unable to provide personal guarantees or collateral to the bank. Brilliant, isn't it? Of course, there is the long process of filling up forms—and be prepared for an extended period of silence, during which no one gets back to you. But then we never said that fundraising was an easy job, did we?

More recently, there is a new scheme for start-ups called MUDRA, or Micro Units Development & Refinance Agency Ltd.[†] Under this scheme, banks and other financial institutions

---

[*] https://www.cgtmse.in/schemes.aspx
[†] www.mudra.org.in

are offered re-finance for loans up to Rs 10 lakh for start-ups and other small units. Incidentally, a number of start-ups have availed of this scheme.

One caveat. Obviously, as a start-up, you cannot get a loan worth crores of rupees. But even a small loan of a few lakhs may help you wade through troubled times—until, of course, you get your big round of equity funding.

Incubators and Accelerators

For the uninitiated—not you, of course—an incubator is a place where chicks are hatched from eggs. Or a specialized area in a hospital where premature babies are supported to ensure they survive and are able to face the world. But hang on. Isn't a start-up a kind of baby, which needs support to survive and face the world? And that's why we now have incubators for start-ups as well. Essentially to provide financial, infrastructural, technical as well as mentoring support to 'baby start-ups'. At an early stage, when start-ups are at a high risk of shutting shop if they do not get support.

Let's tell you a story about incubators. Manoj, an engineer working in the US, dreamt of building software to optimize fuel consumption in small diesel generators and motors. He decided to come back to India and work on his project. Fortunately, he was able to house his project in an incubator within an engineering college. The incubator provided him with all the infrastructure he needed, including access to the laboratories of the college. It also provided him with a soft loan at a highly subsidized interest rate of 8 per cent. And the best part was that he was getting connected to angels, VCs and even potential customers. In fact, the incubator also helped him register his patent. Over the next three years, Manoj built his company from within the incubator and even raised funding from a VC. Finally, when his start-up was ready to face the world, he moved out into his own office. Today Manoj runs a thriving business, and a lot of the credit for this must go to the incubator. And, by the way, stories like this one are becoming more and more common in India these days.

Historically, academic institutions and state counties in the US were the first to set up incubators. These are typically furnished offices with or without other common facilities that are made available to start-ups at subsidized rates. In addition, they provide mentoring and networking that any start-up needs so desperately. As mentioned earlier, some of them also provide equity, debt and even grants to their incubatees. So not only do they give you a small amount of money, but they also help in cutting down your expenses—which brings down your requirement for funding, doesn't it?

Coming to India, many academic institutions have set up incubators—SINE in IIT Bombay, FITT in IIT Delhi and CIIE in IIM Ahmedabad are some of the big guys. In fact, incubators housed in engineering colleges also provide access to labs, to permit entrepreneurs to tinker around with their product. In most cases, Indian incubators permit you to stay for three years—after which they would want you to shift out. After all, you will hopefully become a Maruti or a Reliance someday, and at that stage you wouldn't need an incubator, would you? So you are politely and firmly 'requested' to make way for the next incubatee!

And then we have the other avatar of the incubator—the accelerator. Incubators usually take on start-ups at an early stage and give them lots of time to conceptualize and build their business. On the other hand, accelerators take on start-ups that are already in business and help them scale up rapidly. Typically, accelerators support start-ups for three to six months, and the inputs and mentorship are far more concentrated than those in incubators. At the end of the accelerator programme, investors are invited to pitch sessions as usual.

You must have heard of Y Combinator. If you haven't, you haven't arrived on the start-up circuit yet, so we would strongly urge you to look it up on the net. Perhaps the most famous accelerator worldwide. Based in California (where else?), it has a mouth-watering list of alumni, which includes Dropbox and Airbnb. Many start-ups that go through its programmes have grown into big boys, and several have become unicorns. And then we have the other big accelerator, Techstars. In more recent times, global companies such as Google, Microsoft, Facebook and Intel have also created acceleration programmes for start-ups. Even in India, several companies such as Mahindra & Mahindra, ICICI Bank and Yes Bank have launched accelerator programmes with the intention of nurturing start-ups within their own area of interest.

Grants and Other Goodies from the Government

Meet Dr Anopheles (not his real name, in case you haven't already guessed), the founder of 'Malaria Test'. Doctor sahib was keen to develop a low-cost diagnostic kit to detect malaria. So he set himself up in an incubator and started working on a low-cost diagnostic tool. Unfortunately, while some initial funding was available from the incubator, he needed a lot more to take the project forward. Also, this was a long-gestation project, with revenues far into the future. Which meant that neither angels nor VCs were interested. Dr Anopheles reached a stage where he was literally tearing out his rather sparse hair in frustration. Such a brilliant idea and so useful for the country. All he needed was some money . . .

Fortunately, it didn't take too many strands of his hair to get a solution, which actually came from a mentor. 'Why don't you apply to the government for a grant? For your kind of project, grants are available.' And so our founder-doctor applied for a government grant. But then got into a further bout of frustration and hair-pulling. After all, long-winded government procedures and forms are not designed to make life easy, are they? But finally it happened—he got his grant, with which he was able to kick off the next stage of the project. And then something really interesting happened. Since the project was now close to a launch, angels actually started getting interested.

And at the time of writing this book, Dr Anopheles was likely to get a large round of angel funding.

So grants are available, and should be used wherever possible. Many start-ups are not even aware of them—or are aware but extremely sceptical and therefore don't even apply. That's not a good idea. After all, grants come without any strings attached—there is no dilution of equity and no one asks you to pay back the money. Of course, there is no guarantee you'll get the grant, but what's the harm in applying? Some of the key government agencies in India that give grants are the Department of Science and Technology, or DST, and the Department of Biotechnology, or DBT. More recently, grants are also available from industry associations such as NASSCOM, CII and FICCI. Incidentally, some companies also offer grants, provided your project is of interest to them. Yes, it's a lot of work to get a grant but it's well worth the effort, since it is free money. Just keep one thing in mind. Apply for grants, but don't bank on them. If a grant does come your way, celebrate and treat it as a bonus. But please, please, do not build it into your business plan.

By the way, do you know why the government is so keen to nurture start-ups? It's because smart policymakers have realized that start-ups provide growth in the economy and generate jobs. And all in double quick time with limited capital. Therefore governments across the world—including the Government of India—are going all out to support start-ups. Not only does the government provide grants, it also gives significant tax exemptions to start-ups registered with Startup India. Even several public-sector companies, such as ONGC, Indian Oil and HPCL, have set up funds to promote start-ups. Yes, dear founder, you are being royally pampered. And you must take full advantage of it.

Business Plan Competitions

Ankur and Rohini were third-year students at one of the IITs, and were working on a start-up. What start-up? Actually, that's not relevant, so let's skip the description. What *is* relevant is that they wanted a couple of lakhs to build a rudimentary prototype, based on which they would apply to the incubator at IIT. Now, assuming you have been to college, you are aware that college students do not have cash. So what did they do? Interestingly, they decided to participate in one of several business plan competitions held across India. And guess what? They actually won the third prize and got Rs 50,000. Not enough, but definitely a start. And that gave them hope. So they went full throttle into several business competitions and raised over Rs 3 lakh in the next year. Enough and beyond for the prototype they wanted to build. And yes, they did get into the incubator.

So that's another method of raising money—definitely not in crores, but money is money, after all. The other huge benefit is that these contests give you other goodies such as free mentoring and server space credits, as well as space for doing demos in conferences and expos. They also give you a chance to meet fellow entrepreneurs, and even investors. Several IITs and IIMs hold such contests from time to time. So do some companies such as Lufthansa, IBM and Samsung.

To summarize, issuing shares is not the only way to raise money. There are lots of other ways as well. These may not give you crores—or millions of dollars, if you prefer—but any cash is always welcome, isn't it? So do look around you, and try and get whatever you can.

Section III

Later-Stage Funding

Those Who Made It and Those Who Couldn't

Let's Meet Dinesh Agarwal, Founder and CEO, IndiaMART

One of the biggest success stories of our start-up world has been IndiaMART. As a consumer, you might not have used it, but as a business, you would most definitely have—because it's by far the largest B2B marketplace in India. And unlike many other Internet companies, it has been profitable from its very early days. We caught up with the affable founder, Dinesh Agarwal, and asked him to share some of his insights for the benefit of our readers. This is what he had to say:

> One fundamental question that every entrepreneur needs to ask is, 'What's the kind of business I am building?' All businesses don't have to be billion-dollar businesses. Entrepreneurship is not about one big Facebook. There are thousands and thousands of smaller companies that are doing well, and are profitable. And they may not need external funding—at least for a long time. So first decide what you want to become. The often-used phrase 'Go big or go home' is definitely not valid.

Secondly, and equally importantly, don't chase funding. Chase the business. Focus on profitable growth. Many businesses don't need funding, but the hype in the media as well as peer pressure force you to raise funding. Unfortunately, funding today has become a milestone. In fact, lots of businesses have suffered because of excessive funding.

Gaadi tez chalana ek nasha hai. Lekin jab petrol *khatam ho jaye to kya hoga* (Speeding gives you a thrill, but what happens when you run out of petrol)?

Finally, a few pieces of advice beyond funding. Remember, entrepreneurship is a long journey. And it can be frustrating at times. Be persistent. Keep trying—and you'll get lucky. Also remember, simple solutions can solve big problems. And, finally, pack your team with high-passion people. High-quality people are not enough—high-passion people will help you win.

Wise words, Dinesh. We're sure they will be extremely helpful for potential entrepreneurs. Thanks a lot for sharing your thoughts.

11

The Super Tale of Planet Superheroes

The New Year party was going strong, and the beer was just perfectly chilled. Just the time to let your hair down. But not for Jaineel Aga. No sir, Jaineel was thinking. And no, it was not the kind of thinking that invariably accompanies alcohol. It was serious thinking. And as the night wore on, he began to think some more. And more. Slowly, ever so slowly, the frustration started creeping in: 'What am I doing with my life?' he wondered. And as the beer had its effect, he became more specific: 'What the hell am I doing with my life?'

A few years ago, Jaineel had returned to India from the US, armed with a master's in engineering management from Duke University. And had landed what most of his peers felt was a plum job with a private equity firm. The money was great. In the beginning, so was the learning. But over time, he realized that poring over Excel sheets was not getting him anywhere. He wasn't learning anything new, and with every passing month he felt that his career was going nowhere. And all this came to a head during that fateful New Year's Eve in 2013.

As you will learn in this story, Jaineel was a quick decision maker, and by the morning his mind had been made up. He would quit his job and start his own venture. But doing what—that was the million-dollar question. And that was the beginning of months and months of exploring, thinking, validating and then exploring again. Jaineel was clear that he would do something that he understood—and he understood consumer behaviour. So it would have to be a consumer-centric business. Also, Jaineel was ambitious—whatever he did would need to be on large scale. Perhaps he could even create a new category. Yes, that was it. Jaineel wanted to be a category creator in the huge consumer market that was India. Of course, if it had been proven in the West, so much the better.

And that's when he started zeroing in on merchandise based on comic characters—T-shirts, mugs, keychains, phone covers—all with images of characters such as Superman, Batman, Iron Man, Captain America and Johnny Bravo on them. He found it surprising that in such a huge consumer market, there was no organized, home-grown brand around this theme. Yes, there was the unorganized market, largely sold on pavements, where the quality was highly suspect. T-shirts that would fade rapidly, keychains with poor-quality printing, phone covers with part of the character missing—the list was endless. But there was no organized brand that delivered high-quality stuff, mug after mug, keychain after keychain.

The more Jaineel thought about it, the more he warmed to the theme. Surely there was a huge army of customers out there who were keen to buy good quality, branded stuff? One fine day, while dipping his feet into the sea at the desolate Juhu beach in Mumbai, Jaineel made his decision. And Planet Superheroes, or simply PSH, was born!

The first and most important issue was the comic characters themselves. Jaineel was clear that his business would be entirely ethical and legal. In other words, he needed to get licences to reproduce these characters on the merchandise he planned to sell—for instance, DC Comics for Superman or Marvel for Iron Man. And that meant dollars. Thousands of dollars. Or several lakhs of rupees, if that makes you more comfortable.

Obviously, the first thing to do was to see if he had enough money to at least make a start. This was not the right stage to go to angel investors—after all, it was only an idea so far. And therefore, Jaineel did the most obvious thing. He checked and rechecked his bank accounts, fixed deposits and all the other savings he had put together. He spoke to two friends, who, fortunately, had money as well, and the three of them decided to go ahead with the idea together. Happily, between them there was enough money to get the first few licences—for Johnny Bravo, the Simpsons, Family Guy and Dexter's Laboratory. Of course, you must remember that these licenses came with stringent conditions. First of all, they were only valid for specific categories of merchandise. For instance, a licence for the category 'mugs' would not apply to T-shirts. Secondly, any modifications to the design, such as Johnny Bravo playing cricket— something unheard of in the US—would need to be approved by the licence owner. And finally, all products manufactured would need to be approved by the quality-assurance department of the licensor. But Jaineel was quite happy with these conditions. You see, he was equally concerned about the quality of his products.

Next, of course, Jaineel created a logo and a website, appropriately named Planetsuperheroes.com. He was clear that this was an e-commerce venture, where all sales would be done online. It clearly didn't make sense to invest in physical stores at this stage. Maybe later, but in the beginning it would be e-commerce all the way. And so Planet Superheroes started off on its e-commerce journey. Sales were decent, but so were the expenses. Marketing the brand was a major money guzzler. So were operations, since the products had to be delivered to customers. And over time, the inevitable happened. Of course you know what. The company ran out of funds and needed to raise more. Let's hear it from Jaineel himself:

As an early mover in a niche industry, gaining momentum and mind recall was critical for us. This required up-front investments that were disproportionately higher than the immediate returns. Secondly, since Planet Superheroes was in the business of selling authorized and official merchandise, we needed to pay large royalties up front to even secure a licence. Bootstrapping wouldn't have worked. For both these reasons, external funding was the only way to quickly make a mark.

In very simple terms, Jaineel needed money. Lots of it. And therefore, his next stop was—that's right—angel investors.

The Pitch

The pitch took place in both Mumbai and Delhi. By now, of course, the angels were aware of the PERSISTENT approach and asked very specific questions. Yes, there was a problem that Jaineel was solving. After all, there were lots of people buying merchandise based on comic characters and many were not happy with the quality. But more than a problem, it was an opportunity to tap into the quality-conscious market.

However, there were risks, and that, too, major ones, which the angels raised. First of all, licences for the comic characters were expensive. What if the company were unable to sell in large enough volumes to cover this cost? And then, of course, the competition. Competing with pavement sellers all over the country was not going to be easy. When they had started, a typical T-shirt from Planet Superheroes cost upwards of Rs 600, whereas a poorer-quality product was available on pavements for half the price. And here was the kicker—there would probably be enough quality-conscious customers around, *but they obviously wouldn't care whether or not the character was licensed.* Undoubtedly this was a risk, and Jaineel agreed. However, based on several months of experience in the business so far, he was confident that there was a large enough market for quality products. Further, he mentioned that only licensed products would have the latest designs, and these would take time to copy!

The angels also saw the growth PSH had been able to achieve, and that was certainly impressive. Scalability was also not an issue—

the market was potentially huge and, in any case, e-commerce did not require any significant manual intervention.

But there was one overriding issue that the angels noticed, so please pay attention and listen. And that was the entrepreneur. Jaineel was outstandingly passionate about his business and equally confident. His knowledge of the field and his attention to detail were terrific. Every time the angels asked him a simple question, Jaineel responded with a detailed answer, loaded with facts. And it pushed all the right buttons with the angels. The mood around the table became more and more positive, and Jaineel sensed that the money was about to come in.

Above all, Jaineel was extremely 'PERSISTENT'. In this connection, let's tell you a story. I—the first author of this book—had decided to invest in the company, and therefore had to sign on the shareholder agreement (more about this in Chapter 20). Now I was also scheduled to go abroad for a holiday. And I had clearly told Jaineel that I would be able to sign the document either before going abroad, or after returning. But—and this was made very clear—I was not to be disturbed during the holiday. Jaineel agreed.

Sure enough, on the second day of my holiday, I got a message asking me to sign. I refused. Jaineel persisted. I said I was in a foreign country with major language issues and I'd find it difficult. But Jaineel was adamant—he told me that my hotel would have a printer that I could use to print the document, sign it and then send a photograph. No matter what I said, Jaineel wouldn't budge. Of course, I was equally stubborn and refused to budge either—but you get the message. When Jaineel wanted something, he would push and push till he got it. And that, my friend, is the meaning of the term 'PERSISTENT'!

After the Funding, More Funding

So did Jaineel get his funding? You bet he did. Over three crores of it—or nearly half a million dollars, if you prefer. Some of it from former colleagues from his private equity days, some from the angels and the rest from a major Singapore-based VC called DSG Consumer Partners, headed by the well-known investor Deepak Shahdadpuri. But believe me, it wasn't easy. Let's listen to what Jaineel had to say on the fund raise:

> Raising funds is never easy. It always takes more time than you expect. And till you actually reach the MITB (money in the bank) stage, you are nothing. There are a lot of things that can happen between commitments—even paper commitments—and fruition of the deal.
>
> And, by the way, don't be disheartened when an investor turns you down. Go back to focusing on the customer, keep listening to him and the funding will come.

To get back to the fund raise, now that the money was in, Jaineel started looking at newer ways to increase sales. For a start, he realized that for most customers, his products were an 'impulse purchase'. It was possible that some fans might say, 'Today I'm going to buy a Spiderman T-shirt.' But there was also the other kind. Boy and girl go to a nearby mall for a date. Girl sees a Harry Potter bobblehead displayed in a shop. Girl says, 'Oh, how cute.' Boy, in an attempt to get her to stay with him a bit longer, promptly buys it for her. Boy's father pays. Story over.

But for Jaineel, the story was not over yet. Knowing that impulse purchases were likely to be a large chunk of sales, he had to get his products into physical shops and not just bank on online sales. So he started negotiating with large shops to sell his products through them. But as you are aware, life is never so easy. Shops were willing to take on his products, but they would only pay him for what was sold. The rest would simply be returned. You must remember that PSH was a new player and that these shops were owned by hard-nosed businessmen who had been born and brought up on negotiations. They were adamant and Jaineel had to give in.

So the PSH merchandise started appearing on shop shelves. Sales did pick up, but there was one issue. People did not ask for their products by name. Yes, they would look for T-shirts with comic characters on them. But they wouldn't ask for T-shirts from Planet Superheroes. After all, the brand wasn't yet strong enough to generate this kind of pull. So Jaineel looked at another option, that of 'shop-in-shop'. Now you are obviously a smart reader, so you know what that means. But for those who don't, this is a separate section in a shop, set aside specifically for PSH and its products. Something like a PSH corner. Jaineel created such 'shops-in-shops' in several stores and, once again, it worked. It wasn't that people came in and asked for PSH products. But at least they came in and saw the shop-in-shop. Curious, they would come over to the PSH corner and hopefully some of them would buy their products! And, incidentally, the brand got built up in the process. Terrific, wasn't it?

But hang on. As you are aware, you never get something for nothing. With sales in physical outlets, PSH needed to keep ready stocks at the outlets. With e-commerce, their warehouse was enough, but now, every shop that sold their products had to stock them. And that meant far, far more stocks than before. And that meant—aha, you've got it—far more money to buy and keep these stocks.

And so young Jaineel went back to the familiar money-raising game. As always, it wasn't easy. Fortunately, however, the business was growing rapidly. Most importantly, the confidence that investors had placed in Jaineel during the first round had been vindicated, and they were hungry for more. Jaineel decided to raise a rights issue—aimed at the existing shareholders, including DSG Consumer Partners. And as you might expect, the issue was lapped up and he was able to get nearly a crore and a half in funding. With money no longer an issue, keeping stocks was not a problem, and Jaineel was able to grow his business through physical outlets as well.

But people like Jaineel do not sit back and relax. At least we have never seen him relaxing. They are constantly thinking, 'What next?' And having tasted success in sales through physical outlets, the next step was obvious. That's right, he decided to launch exclusive outlets for Planet Superheroes! Now here he had two options. These outlets could either be owned by the company or they could be in franchise mode. Clearly, creating his own outlets would require a lot of capital, even if he were to rent out the space. Interiors would need to be constructed, salespeople would need to be employed and, above all, lots of stock would need to be maintained. Just imagine the following situation:

Walk-in customer with a girlfriend in tow: 'Do you have this *Game of Thrones* T-shirt in a smaller size?'

Salesperson: 'No sir, but we can get it for you.'

Walk-in customer: 'What about Captain America?'

Salesperson: 'Sir, that may take a few days.'

Walk-in customer (angrily to his girlfriend): 'See, I told you it was a mistake to come here. Let's go and have an ice cream!'

Obviously Jaineel couldn't afford this. And, therefore, maintaining enough stock at each outlet was absolutely vital. Franchising, of course, would require a lot less capital, and no salaries to be paid. Most importantly, if he could get a few franchisees who believed in the brand, he could actually get them to buy the merchandise *on a non-returnable basis.* And the smart reader knows what that means— no stocks to be owned by PSH. And, therefore, much, much less funds required. Obviously this came at a cost—Jaineel would get lower margins, since the risk was now being taken by the franchisees.

The decision was fairly obvious, and Jaineel decided to go for the franchising option. By now, of course, given the growth of sales and the popularity of the Planet Superheroes brand, franchisees were more than willing to come on board. And over the next few months, Jaineel was able to launch four franchised outlets.

By the way, you probably know Jaineel quite well by now. So you can guess what he would do next. And you're dead right. He went ahead and added new licenses that would address the much-ignored pre-school space, such as Peppa Pig and PAW Patrol, to his already-strong portfolio. Which also meant more licence fees, and therefore the need for more funding. And yes, our friend Jaineel was successfully able to raise one more round.

Today Jaineel can sit back and survey his empire with satisfaction—although he rarely sits back. It is now the among the largest character-based merchandise providers in India. And it is omni-channel—through its own portal, over twenty-five physical outlets, leading retail chains such as Hamleys, Toys"R"Us, Mothercare and Trent (from the Tatas), partnerships with multiplexes such as PVR and online marketplaces such as Amazon. Interestingly, Jaineel has recently also added local characters such as Chacha Chaudhary to his already-diversified repertoire, targeting 'Bharat' along with 'India' as they reach out to more customers.

The company has won several start-up awards, including the gold winner twice at Comic Con India, the world-famous event for anything to do with comics and comic characters. And it won't surprise you to know that it has just raised a Series A round of funding, this time adding a marquee Japanese gaming company to its investor base—making it four rounds in all so far.

There is, however, one thing that Jaineel wanted to share with the readers of this book. So in his own words, here it is:

Raising money is never easy. It takes time and lots and lots of patience. Particularly in later-stage funding, when the amounts involved are much higher, investors need a solid amount of convincing. For instance, one of the questions we had to answer repeatedly was, 'This doesn't seem to be a serious business, so why should we invest in it?'

Fortunately, we had DSG Consumer Partners on our side every time. And the interesting thing is that once they agreed, the other investors usually followed—not wanting to be left out. And that was one key thing I learnt. Get one key investor to back you, to champion your cause. And once you've got them on your side, it'll usually lead to others coming in as well.

So that's the story of Planet Superheroes so far. And knowing our young founder, we can safely predict an even brighter future for him and his company. An investor's delight.

And, by the way, if you are keen to invest in PSH, let us know—we'll put you in touch with Jaineel.

Analysis

As you can imagine, dear reader, Planet Superheroes is the kind of company investors dream of. Large MARKET SIZE and a great founder to exploit it. With an ENTRY BARRIER built over time in the form of quality and, therefore, the brand. SCALABILITY was not an issue, since it was a product and not a service business and, therefore, not dependent on a huge manpower.

Yes, the presence of pavement markets selling low-quality stuff at half the price was a RISK, but isn't that true of any business? Name any product—from clothing to room coolers and heaters—and you will always have a situation where branded, quality products are competing with cheaper, unbranded ones. And there are enough customers for both kinds!

At this point, we'd like to mention one extremely important issue. All along, we have been talking about the PERSISTENT approach. Now, in early-stage investing, the investor looks at the *likelihood* of the business being PERSISTENT. And is willing to take a risk with it. But at later stages, typically when VCs come in, they will not invest on hope. No way. They want to see results. They want hard numbers.

Have you been able to SCALE up rapidly?
Is there far more TRACTION than before?

Has your burn been coming down—and therefore have you proved your EARNINGS MODEL?

You see? Early-stage investors look at the future, because there is very little past. But *later-stage investors look at the past, in addition to the future*. In Jaineel's case, they liked what they saw. And so the dollars (or rupees, if you prefer) flowed in . . .

Finally, what does our PERSISTENT table look like? Here it is:

The PERSISTENT Approach Applied to Planet Superheroes

	Issue	Planet Superheroes
P	**PROBLEM:** Are you solving a real problem? Will people pay?	More than a problem, this was an opportunity.
E	**EARNINGS MODEL**	Revenue from the sale of merchandise. Unit economics positive.
R	**RISKS** and how you will mitigate them	By ensuring quality and therefore differentiating PSH from the unorganized market.
S	**SIZE OF THE MARKET**	Very large.
I	**INNOVATION**	-
S	**SCALABILITY**	Not an issue, since it was a product and not a service industry.
T	**TEAM**, starting with the founders	Extremely passionate, confident and knowledgeable founder. Very PERSISTENT.
E	**ENTRY BARRIERS**	Licences as well as quality. Over time, also the brand.
N	**NICHE:** When the market is crowded, identify a niche	A large-enough niche of branded, character-based merchandise.
T	**TRACTION**	At every stage of funding, Jaineel was able to show higher traction.

12

The Phenomenal Success Story of Cashify

Cashify is the fascinating story of three friends—Nakul Kumar, Mandeep Manocha and Amit Sethi. It's different from many of the other stories in this book, because it talks about a company that has already made it big. A major brand and a market leader in its field. And growing every month . . .

But let's start from the beginning. Mandeep and Nakul had completed their bachelor's degree in engineering from Punjab University, after which Mandeep went to National Institute of Industrial Engineering (NITIE), Mumbai, and Nakul went to Management Development Institute (MDI), Gurgaon, to study management. Now, post their management degrees, you might imagine that both friends picked up the inevitable jobs that all good MBAs do. And lived happily ever after.

No sir. Our young friends were clear that they were destined for something far better than miserable 9–11 jobs. (Of course, you are aware that 9–5 jobs do not exist any more. They were only there during your grandfathers' time.) They simply had to do something on their own. And so, over a chilled-beer session one warm summer evening, they started thinking. And the thinking went on and on (along with the beer, of course—remember, nothing perks up the grey cells like alcohol). Looking for a large opportunity in the Indian market. And suddenly, while disposing of one of the empty beer bottles, it hit them. Yes, you're right, the empty beer bottle provided the inspiration. Why not look at waste management? What a huge opportunity that would be!

And that, ladies and gentlemen, was the start of a long, arduous and often frustrating journey. Remember, building a company is not easy. At the best of times it's a 24x7 commitment, and it requires mountains of patience. But, of course, you already know this. For four long years, our friends Nakul and Mandeep experimented with a variety of projects in waste management. They tried out and discarded different business models. They even took up consulting projects in the area, just to understand waste management better. They certainly did not have it easy. Fortunately, there was light at the end of the tunnel. And they finally zeroed in on the rapidly growing area of electronic waste—the zillions of laptops and printers and mobile phones and . . .

Interestingly, they realized that a lot of the so-called electronic waste, such as used laptops, was not actually waste. It could easily be reused. Lots of people would dispose of their old laptops, but lots of other people were happy to buy them—provided, of course, they worked. Our friends quickly decided that this was to be their business. Buy second-hand laptops, check them to see if they were functioning, repair them where possible and resell them. Hopefully for a higher price. An interesting business, popularly known as 'recommerce'.

And what about the name of the company? Here our founders had an interesting idea. Remember, they were picking up second-hand laptops from users. And giving those users cash in return. In other words, they were helping users convert their laptops to cash. So why not call the company 'Cashify'? The more the two thought about it, the more they warmed to the theme. And so, with the appropriate beating of drums and blowing of trumpets, Cashify was born. By the way, at this stage they also realized that technology

124   Funding Your Start-Up

would play a large part in their business. And therefore they needed a person with a technical background to join them, for which they roped in a friend, Amit Sethi, as co-founder.

Having decided on the name as well as the business model, the next step was to put the idea into operation. Since all of them were Delhi-based, they started buying second-hand laptops from Nehru Place, which was the hub of the second-hand electronic market in Delhi—albeit completely unorganized. After checking and repairing these laptops where necessary, our friends would sell them online— through their contacts. And that was the start of Cashify's business in Delhi and Gurgaon, in 2013. Simple, wasn't it?

Well, not really. What our young founders realized was this: While there was a huge demand for used laptops, supply was a problem. Unorganized markets like Nehru Place were highly unprofessional and unreliable. To understand this, let's listen in to a typical conversation between a shop owner in Nehru Place and his *mundu*, or helper.

Mundu: '*Sirjee, woh Cashify wale phir aaye hain* (Sir, those people from Cashify are here again).'

Shop owner (sounding like Gabbar Singh): '*Kitne laptop chahiye* (How many laptops do they want)?'

Mundu: '*S-s-sirjee, bees laptop* (S-s-sir, twenty laptops).'

Shop owner: '*Hmm . . . Bees laptop . . . Hmm . . . Aur pichhli baar* (Hmm . . . Twenty laptops . . . Hmm . . . And what about last time)?'

Mundu: '*S-sirjee, teen laptop* (S-sir, three laptops).'

Shop owner (with a cunning look): '*Theek hai. Unko bol do aajkal market mein second-hand laptop nahin hain. Daam pehle se bees per cent zyaada lagega* (Okay. Tell them second-hand laptops are in short supply in the market. The rate will be 20 per cent higher now).'

So you get the idea, don't you? Unprofessional suppliers that Cashify simply couldn't rely on. And you can imagine what that did to the carefully made Excel sheets and cash-flow statements of the two entrepreneurs. Further, there was no guarantee on the models that were available. Much of the time there were only a few models in stock, which meant the options Cashify could make available to their buyers were limited. In the process, they might actually lose buyers. The other key issue was that such unreliable supplies made scalability difficult. And without scalability, what was the point of running a small, slowly growing business?

What was the option? Actually there was only one option—buy directly from the user who wanted to sell his laptop, rather than from the intermediary. And, therefore, our founders created a website where they would do both—buy from a user and sell to another user. Initially they started off by employing a person who would do a home pick-up as well as delivery, but then they realized this was not really viable unless the volumes were massive. So they decided to partner with companies that were in the logistics space and were delivering large volumes anyway. These partners would pick up laptops from the sellers' homes and bring them to Cashify. They would also deliver laptops to the buyers' homes.

So the business continued. And grew. But our young founders were fidgety. The opportunity in this business seemed so large, and what they had tapped was just so small. It didn't make sense. They had a huge opportunity facing them, and they wanted to grow the business even more rapidly, by spreading to other cities. But for that they needed money. How else would they maintain an inventory of saleable, used laptops? How else would they reach out to buyers as well as sellers across the country? How else would they set up testing and repair facilities across India? How else would they . . .

But you get the idea, don't you? In very simple, blunt terms, they needed money.

The Funding and After

Interestingly, our friends first tried to get a bank loan. But that didn't work out. As you know, banks usually need collateral against which they give loans (the situation has changed a bit now, with collateral-free loans such as the government's MUDRA loan, but these only provide small amounts of funding). So what collateral could Cashify offer? They didn't have a factory, they didn't have plant and machinery. What they had was lots of second-hand laptops. But who would value them? The bank wanted collateral that someone had officially valued. Only then could they give loans against it. But there was no way to value second-hand laptops. And therefore the bank-loan story died a quiet, peaceful, completely natural death.

But our friends still required money, so they started looking at the equity option. They spoke to several angel investors but, once again, the response was not particularly encouraging.

'Second-hand laptops? How will you compete with the "Nehru Places" of the world?'

'Is this really a large potential business?'

'Repairs, pickup, delivery—too operations-heavy.'

'Can you make money?'

And so on. Lots of questions but no money. Interestingly, a couple of angels told them that for the kind of operations-heavy business they were running, they would need far more funding than angels could provide. And so our friends started approaching VCs as well. But once again, the objections were the same and the response poor. No funding.

Now what happened next was very important, so make sure you are awake and reading very, very carefully. No dozing off, please. Since funding was not forthcoming, *our friends decided to stop chasing investors and focus on the business instead.* Grow it with whatever money they had. Equally important, since there was no money coming in, they had to make the business profitable. Otherwise it would simply die.

And that, ladies and gentlemen, was perhaps the turning point in the Cashify story. Since they had no funding, the founders did not attempt to grow ten times. Instead, they focused on the business and attempted to make it grow profitably, even though it would be at a slower pace. Now since they were not looking at stupendous growth, they did not need funding, at least for the moment. So they stopped meeting investors and instead focused full-time on the business. And the battle continued . . .

Finally, at the end of 2014, something fascinating happened. By now the business had grown and had also become profitable. And believe it or not, the VCs actually came back. Yes, you heard that right—the same VCs who had turned up their noses at the opportunity earlier. On their own, without Cashify going to them. *So now it wasn't Cashify chasing the VCs, it was the VCs chasing Cashify.* Simply because the company had proved that it was following a viable business model, it was profitable and, most of all, it had shown some growth—or traction, as investors like to call it. And so there was a fairly-tale wedding—Cashify was able to raise half a million dollars from two VCs—Blume Ventures and Bessemer Venture Partners. And with this, the future had opened up for them.

At this stage, it's interesting to hear Nakul's views on the subject of funding:

> Funding cannot be your goal. Funding is a means to achieving your business goals. Do you celebrate when you get a bank loan? Of course not! So why do you celebrate when you get equity funding? Unfortunately, the media measures the success of a company by the rounds of funding they have raised, as well as the valuations. And founders are very happy to follow suit. But isn't that silly? What will you do with funding if your business does not pick up?
>
> And, by the way, if your business is dependent on funding, you are in the wrong business. Your business needs to be

viable on its own. Funding should only be a means to generate higher growth.

Wise words from a wise founder.

Incidentally, around this time, namely 2014, something else happened. As you are aware, by this time the mobile-phone market in India was beginning to explode. And with the company becoming so successful with used laptops, why not try out used phones as well? They did exactly that, and the Cashify growth story boomed further, given that the volumes involved were so much higher. And so it went on.

We must also tell you something else that our founders focused on. Right from the beginning, they were clear that they were not a run-of-the-mill repair shop. They were a highly innovative, technology-driven company, far, far removed from the unorganized repair market in Nehru Place and Ghaffar Market (another place for repaired second-hand goods in Delhi). Automation was the name of the game, right from their entire supply chain to the diagnostic software they had developed for mobile phones. This was their entry barrier, and this is what would ultimately take them to a leadership position in the market.

You may have heard of an old saying, 'Success begets success.' And that's what happened to Cashify. Having grown successfully after raising their first round from VCs, the founders were able to raise three more rounds, each at a higher valuation compared to the previous round. And they used the funding to grow and grow. Interestingly, during one of these rounds, in 2017, they also got in a strategic investor from China—AiHouShou—a giant in the recommerce space. Which quite naturally beefed up their ambitions of foraying beyond India. They also launched their own refurbished brand of phones called Phone Pro, and another brand, Screen Pro, in which they repaired smartphone screens on the spot, at customers' homes.

Today Cashify has a swanky office in the heart of Gurgaon, and at the time of writing this book, does business involving more than a lakh of devices of various kinds every month. Just to give you an idea of their phenomenal growth, just a year ago they were doing 50,000 devices per month. In other words, even at this size, they have achieved significant growth of 2X in just this past one year. And the previous year was even more unbelievable, because they grew from 5,000 to 50,000 devices—a truly staggering growth of 10X. They work with multiple brands and operate through fourteen hubs across the country—each with its own warehouse and testing and repair centre. Interestingly, while they buy used phones directly from the user, they now sell only through retailers. In other words, they are solving the supply problem for retailers of used phones.

Cashify has truly 'cashed in' on the increasing aspiration levels of young India. There is data to show that smartphone users seem to want the latest models, and the lifespan of ownership is just over a year. And in this kind of market, is it surprising that Cashify has grown the way it has? Yes, ladies and gentlemen, Cashify has been one of the major success stories of the start-up world. Let's learn from it.

Analysis

This analysis is simple, isn't it? These guys check perhaps all the boxes in our PERSISTENT framework. Huge MARKET SIZE, a solid ENTRY BARRIER built through their brand, INNOVATIVE use of technology as well as their widespread network. Plus, of course, a highly experienced, focused and passionate TEAM of founders. Interestingly, their initial business model was based on buying used laptops from markets such as Nehru Place, which made SCALING UP difficult. But once they had moved to buying laptops and phones directly from consumers, SCALABILITY was not an issue any more. Which tells you once again that business models need to be pivoted, perhaps several times, till you find the magic mix.

At this point, we'd like to revisit something we shared with you when we had discussed Planet Superheroes in the previous chapter. As mentioned, Cashify had raised several rounds of funding.

And each investor would have examined the company within something like our PERSISTENT framework. That much is known. But in each round, the investor would have asked for more and more proof of the PERSISTENT model being followed. Proof of SCALABILITY, TRACTION and the EARNINGS MODEL. Remember, therefore, early-stage companies need to show promise but later-stage ones need to show actuals. Promise alone will not do.

Now there are two additional issues we'd like to highlight here. First of all, notice that Cashify could not raise funds initially. But they did not give up, and instead decided to focus on their business. The business grew and, as if by magic, the investors reappeared. And that's a message to all of you young start-up founders out there. Focus on your business and make it viable. Once that happens, you don't need to chase investors. Hopefully investors will chase you. And you can play hard to get. Just as your girl friend (or boy friend) does.

Secondly, does this story remind you of one of our earlier stories? No? Just go back to the story about SQRRL in Chapter 4. Surely you remember that SQRRL did not get their funding from angel investors. The amount they needed was beyond the reach of angels, and therefore the first round of funding itself came from VCs. Just as it did in the case of Cashify. Yes, ladies and gentlemen, as we have been telling you, in this business there are no rules. In most cases, you would first go to angels for funding. But if you have a significantly larger requirement, you may need to skip the angel stage and go to VCs directly.

Finally what does our PERSISTENT table look like?

The PERSISTENT Approach Applied to Cashify

	Issue	Cashify
P	**PROBLEM:** Are you solving a real problem? Will people pay?	Yes. Buying and selling second-hand devices such as laptops and mobile phones.
E	**EARNINGS MODEL**	Clear. Revenue from the sale of a device minus the cost of the device. Unit economics positive.
R	**RISKS** and how you will mitigate them	-
S	**SIZE OF THE MARKET**	Huge.
I	**INNOVATION**	Extensive use of technology, including diagnostic software for phones.
S	**SCALABILITY**	Highly scalable, after the founders started buying used laptops and phones directly from users.
T	**TEAM**, starting with the founders	Qualified, experienced, clear-headed and passionate founders.
E	**ENTRY BARRIER**	The brand and distribution network—both of which were built over time.
N	**NICHE:** When the market is crowded, identify a niche	
T	**TRACTION**	Significant sales by the time they got their funding.

13

One-Way Trips at One-Way Fares with AHA Taxis

Amit Grover was getting frustrated. He was planning to travel from Delhi to Ludhiana, but train tickets were not available, so he needed a taxi. The local taxi operator was willing to provide a taxi, on condition that Amit took the same taxi both ways. Now Amit had no idea when he would return, and did not want to hang on to the taxi indefinitely. Quite naturally, therefore, he wanted a one-way taxi. The operator was okay with this, but he was clear—the charge would remain the same, whether Amit took the cab one-way or both ways.

Amit was stumped. This did not make sense, and he said so. The taxi operator explained patiently that every outstation taxi had a base city—Delhi, Guwahati, Ludhiana, Coimbatore, etc. Importantly, this taxi could only be hired from its base city. So a Delhi taxi could only be hired from Delhi and a Ludhiana taxi from Ludhiana. In other words, if Amit took a Delhi taxi to Ludhiana and left it there, the taxi would not be able to get a passenger for the return journey. And therefore, continued the operator as if speaking to an imbecile, outstation taxis had no option but to charge two-way or return fare, even if the passenger wished to travel only in one direction.

Amit was not one to give up easily, so he went online. Sure enough, the problem was the same. You were free to travel one way— no one could force you to travel both ways, at least in a democracy like India—but you still had to pay a two-way fare.

Our friend Amit had no choice, so he took the taxi one way and paid the return fare. But he was thinking, 'This must be a common problem. Lots of people need to make one-way trips. Some people might want to stay at their destination for several days and would not want to hang on to their taxis and pay the requisite daily charge for so many days.' Others, like Amit, might not be aware of the duration of their visit. Still others might have got a one-way train ticket but were badly waitlisted on the return journey . . .

The possibilities were endless, but the fundamental issue remained the same. Lots and lots of people wanted one-way outstation taxis, but these were simply not available. And by the time Amit reached Ludhiana, an idea had begun to take shape in his mind. Was this a business opportunity? Could he connect with taxis that had travelled away from their base cities, and therefore provide them with passengers on the way back? Would taxi operators agree? Could he become an aggregator for one-way taxi services? How would the business work? Could he actually charge one-way fare?

Amit returned to Delhi with barely suppressed excitement. So much so that he even ignored his favourite tandoori chicken when it was placed before him at the dining table. It was clear that a huge number of trips were made in India every day. It was also clear that a significant chunk of them were one-way trips but at two-way fares. He shared his idea with a couple of friends, and they were equally excited. And so AHA Taxis, the inter-city aggregator was born— one-way trips at one-way fares!

The next step, of course, was to figure out how it would work. The founders were clear that bookings would be done online, just as they were in Uber and Ola Cabs. And that required a website. On the website, a potential customer would select his starting city as well as the destination city, along with the date and time of travel.

And, of course, the inevitable category of car—whether a hatchback or a sedan or even an SUV (as you might expect, Ferraris and Rolls-Royces were excluded from the initial launch). So the company had now got full details of the customer's proposed trip.

And now came the tricky part. The company would need to be in touch with taxis to figure out if there was one available for the trip the customer wanted to make. For this, the company first divided the country into routes. For instance, Bombay to Pune was a route, Bombay to Nasik another route, Lucknow to Kanpur a third route, etc. It had also managed to enrol a large number of taxi operators, each operating from a base city and therefore covering routes that included that base city. When a customer wanted to travel on a particular route, for instance from Lucknow to Kanpur, AHA Taxis would send an SMS to all operators who operated on that route. Sometimes they would also call them to speed up the process. Operators would then get back and indicate whether they had a taxi available at the starting city, along with a quote for that particular trip. Based on these quotes, AHA Taxis would select one of the operators, assign the trip to it and inform the passenger. Of course, if the passenger wanted a return trip, that was also available, but obviously at two-way fare.

Now here the intelligent reader (such as you) would have noticed a problem. When the customer wanted to book a taxi, he would obviously need to know the price immediately. How else would he compare prices with other taxis or even aggregators, and therefore decide on which one to take? But the quote from the taxi operators would take time; so how would AHA Taxis give the customer a price and still make money?

As the intelligent reader (you again) would have guessed, the company solved this problem by using past data. They knew how much operators had quoted for each route in the past. They also knew how these quotations varied depending on the day of the week, or even the season. For instance, holiday-season rates were typically higher than normal, because taxis were scarce during this period. So they built a database of rates for every route, with variations for days and seasons. When a customer wanted to book a taxi, the software would automatically check past quotes from the database, add a margin and therefore create a price to be charged to the customer. The key, therefore, was to get lots of data on trips, so that the price given to the customer became more and more accurate and therefore did not eat into the margins of AHA Taxis. And, by the way, as you can guess, this would also create an entry barrier for competitors. Because only companies with lots of past data would be able to forecast quotes accurately and therefore price their trips for customers. Competitors who were new to this business would take time to build this database.

As you can imagine, the concept was lapped up by customers. This was a genuine problem that the company was solving, and their trips kept increasing every month. Very soon they reached a figure of a thousand trips per month and seemed poised to grow beyond this.

But there was a snag. That's right, they needed funding! For operations, for marketing and, of course, for constantly refining their product. And so they made their inevitable visit to angel investors.

The Pitch

And now the story gets really interesting. The first set of angels they went to were unimpressed. 'Tough to implement', 'Not really scalable' and 'Come back after you've got some more traction' were some of the comments the founders heard. They were not really willing to give Amit and gang a chance.

But that was not the end of the story. The founders pitched the idea to a second set of angels, and these angels were genuinely impressed. Most of all with the passion and zeal of the founders. All the founders had come to the pitch session with identical red T-shirts with the AHA Taxis logo prominently displayed. Listening to them, the angels got the impression that the founders really believed in their story. Further, they were really focused on the business at hand. And best of all was their ground-level know-how. They could even recount in precise detail what had happened with their taxi operators even in small towns such as Kalka, Manali and Coonoor. Above all, Amit seemed to be a natural, persuasive leader. Just the right kind of person to take the company forward. Of course, the fact that he was an IIT and IIM alumnus did nothing to dampen the enthusiasm of the investors.

We've said it before, but we'll say it again—the second bunch of angels was impressed. Clearly, this was a problem waiting to be solved. And it was potentially a huge market—after all, outstation taxis were commonly used both for business and personal travel. Of course, there were questions. 'What would you do if one of the huge intra-city operators such as Uber or Ola were to get into your business?' was the first. But Amit was ready with the answer. 'Our entry barrier will be our fleet of inter-city taxi operators. The larger that is, the tougher it will be for the next person to replicate. As of now, Uber is purely into intra-city cabs and Ola is experimenting with the inter-city market. In case either of them plans to get into our business seriously, they will first need to catch up with the size of our fleet. Sure, they will have the money power but getting together a large network of inter-city taxis, and that, too, across the country, will take time. Further, we have the advantage of past data, and therefore our pricing will be very competitive. So, as you can see, we do have entry barriers and these will only grow with time.'

'What about scalability?' asked another angel. 'Finding an appropriate taxi for a given customer seems to be a largely manual process. You need to speak to several operators and then take a call. That's not really scalable.'

'You're right,' said Amit. 'But we are moving towards a more automated solution. And, by the way, that's one reason why we need funding—to take care of the development of this solution.'

Now, at this stage, the curious reader might ask, 'What is this solution?'

Patience, dear reader, patience. Just wait for a bit, and you'll get your answer!

And so the questioning went on. Until finally, after all the grilling, AHA Taxis managed to get its funding. This is what Amit had to say after the funding:

> AHA Taxis started as a bootstrapped venture, from some of the funds and resources we had generated from my previous venture, Nurture Talent Academy. However, considering the enormity of the problem we wanted to address, it was clear at the outset that it would take a lot of investment before reaching sustainability. We could have chosen to run a small shop as a travel agent and still made money in the taxi business, but our dream was to solve something larger for India. And build a system that was perhaps as large as the Indian Railways. That's why we went in for funding.
>
> But we realized one thing—funding is a full-time job. And I was managing both the fund raise as well as the operations. In hindsight, perhaps I should have delegated operations to someone and focused on the fund raise.

Anyhow, to get back to the fund raise, having got his money, a smiling Amit sat back in his office with a cup of coffee to dream and plan (not beer—that's not very conducive to planning, even though it might be highly appropriate for dreaming). Life was looking good, and he began to dream of becoming the king of inter-city taxis in the country. Maybe even beyond the country.

However, we cannot dream. We need to get back to this book and understand what happened after this funding. So read on . . .

After the Funding

Having got the money in the bank, Amit and gang swung into action—not that they weren't swinging earlier. AHA Taxis grew dramatically in the next year—both in terms of the number of taxi operators and the trips made. As they did so, their database of past trips kept improving, and so did their ability to accurately predict quotes from taxi operators. If you recall, this made their margins more predictable and increased their entry barrier.

And now something really interesting happened. Amit needed a second round of funding and happened to go back to the angels who had rejected his proposal earlier. But now he had proved that the market had accepted his business model—something that we call a *product market fit*. He had shown traction and was on the way to building a solid brand. This time the angels were impressed. And what do you think they did? Yes sir, they put in their money—but obviously at a higher valuation than the first round. Incidentally, the earlier angels who had invested in him participated in this round as well—so Amit was able to get a solid chunk of funding.

We caught up with Amit once again and asked him for his key learnings:

> The angels who had rejected us earlier did so because they did not believe in the business model. But when we went back to them, we had proved that it was viable—we had shown growth—and that's why they were happy to invest. And that's a key bit of learning for us—never give up. Keep on building your business and the investors will come. Visualize what you want to achieve in your venture without keeping funding as a constraint. If you do that, you will be able to convince investors to sign their cheques. Don't say, 'Give me the money, and I will do X.' Say 'I will do X, give me the money.'

And with this fresh round of funding, Amit went into overdrive. He realized that his business model could be copied by another aggregator and he needed to remain a step ahead. Specifically, he realized that too much time and manpower was going into the process of identifying taxis that could travel on a particular route once the customer asked for it. Remember, the company would typically make phone calls to operators, get their response and then take a decision on which taxi to take. That took time and manpower, and was therefore costly. So the company worked on an interesting option. Knowing that most of their taxi operators had smartphones, AHA Taxis developed an app that each operator was asked to download. Whenever a customer requested a quote for a particular route, the system automatically sent out requests to all potential operators. This request appeared on the app of each operator, based on which he would quote. The system then automatically selected the operator based on the quotes received. In other words, the company had perfected a 'bidding system', which the operators used to bid for trips.

Notice the improvement over the earlier system. No human intervention, no phone calls. A far more efficient system, both in terms of time and cost. Remember, technology is low-cost and getting lower by the day, whereas humans are expensive and getting more expensive all the time (fortunately for those of us who are salaried). And, quite naturally, the scalability of the business improved because the dependence on people went down. Also note the fact that this had created an additional entry barrier—anyone wishing to get into the same business would need to develop and implement a bidding system, which would take time.

There is something else we must mention. One of the things that set these guys apart from many other start-ups was their phenomenal focus on cost control. As all of you are aware, start-ups do not have money. And therefore it becomes imperative to manage costs. Let us tell you a story about our first visit to the office of AHA Taxis. The office was located on the third floor of a commercial building in Noida, adjoining Delhi. When we reached this building and took the lift to the third floor, we looked for a board, but couldn't find it. So we called up Amit, who told us it was the fifth door on the left. We found the fifth door, entered and immediately saw the smiling faces of Amit and his team.

Our first question to Amit was, 'Why don't you put up a board? How will people find your office?'

Amit's answer really hit us. 'Why should we? No customer will ever come here. They'll only contact us through our website or call up our customer-support number. The only people who'll come here are our taxi operators. And they are regulars, so they know the office. Why should we waste money on a board?'

And that, dear reader, is cost control. All companies need to control their costs, but start-ups need to do so even more. Spend on essentials such as salaries and marketing costs but save wherever it doesn't impact the business. Run your business frugally!

As you might have guessed, over time, AHA Taxis became known as a leader in one-way inter-city taxis. By the way, they also offered two-way taxis, although their rates here were similar to those of competitors. Quite naturally, this brought in the large travel portals such as MakeMyTrip and Yatra. As you are aware, these portals provide all services related to travel, such as air tickets, train tickets and hotel bookings. Clearly, it made sense for them to tie up with AHA Taxis as partners for taxi booking, which is what they did.

As a consequence, AHA Taxis grew and grew. At the time of writing this book, the number of trips per month had increased from a modest single-digit figure to an impressive five-digit figure. They have now partnered with more than 25,000 taxi operators and operate from 4,500 towns and cities. And the growth story continues . . .

But now, dear reader, we need to discuss a very, very important issue. An issue that has to do with risk. What if a huge player with plenty of funding were to get into the space occupied by AHA Taxis? It could be an existing player in intra-city cabs such as Ola or Uber. In fact, at the time of writing this book, Ola was already in the inter-city market, although this was not really a focus area. Or what if it were someone from a completely unrelated area, but with very deep pockets? What if this person were to say, 'Inter-city cabs seem like a good opportunity. Maybe we should get into it.' What happens to our friend, Amit Grover?

If you think this is a risk, you're absolutely right. But if you think this is an opportunity, you are really smart.

Why?

Look at it this way. If a large player wanted to get into this space, they would have essentially two options. Either to grow from scratch, which would take time. Remember, Amit had an established business with 25,000 taxi operators and a robust bidding system. He also had lots of data on past trips. The new, large player could replicate all this, but that would take time. The other option, of course, was to buy a large chunk of shares in AHA Taxis, with Amit and his gang continuing to run it, and thereby avoid the long delays in building up the business from scratch. Something that we call a strategic investment.

And this is exactly what happened to AHA Taxis. Enter eBix Software, the well-known US-based company with the kind of deep pockets we have spoken about. eBix was keen to enter the Indian market and invest in travel-related businesses. They zeroed in on AHA Taxis and decided to take it over early in 2019. By the way, they have also acquired Mercury Travels and Yatra.com and are, therefore, well on the way to becoming a giant in the travel space. So, today, AHA Taxis is known as 'AHA Taxis—an initiative of eBixcash'. No funding issues any more. Whatever they need for growth is made available. And, therefore, our friend Amit's dreams have got even bigger than before.

Incidentally, there was one interesting benefit of the eBix acquisition: eBix had huge contacts in the corporate world and Amit decided to use these contacts. He, therefore, moved from being a pure B2C player to one that operated in both the B2C and the B2B space. In other words, he now provides inter-city taxis to corporate clients as well. By the way, that's another advantage of a strategic investor—you get access to all their contacts.

So the next time you need to travel, please remember to book an AHA Taxi. We believe your experience will be great—Amit will take care of it. And in the process, you will be helping him achieve his dream.

Wish you a very pleasant trip . . .

Analysis

So that was all about AHA Taxis. A rapidly growing company with two successful rounds of funding from angel investors. And finally a strategic investment by eBix Software. Let's analyse the company within our favourite PERSISTENT framework.

Clearly there was a need for this kind of service. There were lots of people who needed one-way taxis but were forced to pay two-way fares. So there was a genuine, widespread PROBLEM. And obviously people were willing to pay—because they ended up saving money. Also, SIZE OF THE MARKET was not an issue. It was potentially huge—given the size and population of our country. Plus, with the economy growing rapidly, business as well as holiday travel would also go up.

One issue—outstation taxis are a crowded space, with a neighbourhood taxi stand in every locality. However, Amit had been smart and had identified a large enough NICHE within this crowded space—namely one-way taxis at one-way fares. Had he simply offered taxis at regular two-way fares, he would not have been able to compete with local operators.

The next issue was SCALABILITY. Initially there was significant manual involvement—which impacted scalability. But over time, Amit introduced a bidding system that partially automated the process of identifying potential taxis for each customer request. And therefore made it easier to scale up.

Further, when the company started off, there was no real ENTRY BARRIER—anyone could have entered this business. But over time, they were able to build up a network of over 25,000 taxi operators across most cities in India. So when a customer wanted a cab, AHA Taxis was very likely to have cabs available from several operators—which the new entrant might not. That, my friend, was his ENTRY BARRIER. Which would only grow with time, as taxi operators spoke to their friends and roped them in as well. Plus, of course, the automated bidding system, which new entrants would need to build—and that would give him a further advantage of a couple of months. And that's a very important issue. Any ENTRY BARRIER buys you some time, after which another player can copy you. Therefore you need to keep raising your ENTRY BARRIER to stay ahead. Therefore, dear founder, if you ever thought you could sit back and relax, just forget it—and enjoy your start-up.

Of course, there was always the RISK of a huge player entering the same space and squeezing out AHA Taxis through discounting. But Amit turned this into an opportunity by creating an INNOVATIVE bidding system for taxi operators and using this to grow rapidly and build a brand. In other words, by becoming an attractive acquisition target, which was then lapped up by eBix.

And, of course, we cannot end without talking about Amit the ENTREPRENEUR. Highly qualified, extremely focused, very passionate about his business and a great leader. What more could anyone ask for?

Finally, please remember that one set of angels had said no to Amit when he had first approached them. But when he showed growth and proved his business model, they were happy to invest. What's the message you get from this? Simple—never give up. As a wise man once said, 'Isn't it strange? The harder I try, the luckier I get.' So keep trying, and you'll get lucky.

And now for our inevitable PERSISTENT table, turn the page:

The PERSISTENT Approach Applied to AHA Taxis

	Issue	AHA Taxis
P	**PROBLEM:** Are you solving a real problem? Will people pay?	One-way inter-city taxis at one-way fares.
E	**EARNINGS MODEL**	A percentage of the amount charged for each trip.
R	**RISKS** and how you will mitigate them	Possibility of a huge player such as Ola Cabs or Uber entering their space. Mitigated to some extent by becoming an attractive acquisition target.
S	**SIZE OF THE MARKET**	Very large.
I	**INNOVATION**	App-based bidding system.
S	**SCALABILITY**	Large market. Manual intervention initially, but automation over time led to improved scalability.
T	**TEAM**, starting with the founders	Founder highly focused, passionate about his business, very persuasive, didn't give up.
E	**ENTRY BARRIERS**	Over time, a large pool of taxi operators, as well as past data on trips. Also their bidding system.
N	**NICHE:** When the market is crowded, identify a niche	One-way inter-city taxis, which is a large enough niche.
T	**TRACTION**	Significant traction over time—which led to the eBix acquisition.

14

Loans for Hospitalization from Uno Finance

The situation was serious. Sandeep's father needed to undergo knee-replacement surgery. Quite naturally, the family wanted the best surgeon and the best hospital, but equally naturally these were exorbitantly priced. And if you were to go into the family's finances, quite simply they were short of money at the moment. Yes, Sandeep was earning well, and over time the money would come in, but at the moment it just wasn't there. What about insurance, you might ask? Well, they did have insurance but, unfortunately, this was what the insurance company called a 'pre-existing condition'. In other words, the problem had been there before they got their insurance and therefore wasn't covered by their policy. So the family had no choice. They begged and borrowed and somehow managed to raise the money, so they were ultimately able to go ahead with the surgery.

Now Sandeep had a close friend, Tushar Aggarwal, who was like a member of the family. When the operation was over and Tushar was walking out of hospital, he looked around him idly and noticed a huge hoarding nearby: 'Buy your favourite SUV in easy instalments.' He looked around further, and there were more such hoardings, all promising easy EMI-based financing options for just about anything you wanted to buy—a home, TVs, laptops, even foreign vacations. And that's when it hit him. There was financing available for just about anything you might want to buy, but not for hospitalization. Health insurance did exist but many families were not covered. Many, many people were not even aware of health insurance. Even among those who were, health insurance was not a priority. 'We don't see any possibility of hospitalization, so there doesn't seem to be any point in wasting money—let's see' was the common refrain. Even for those who had taken insurance policies, the amount covered was woefully inadequate. Unfortunately, therefore, when hospitalization did occur, these people were strapped for cash.

Gradually, ever so slowly, an idea started taking shape in Tushar's mind. Could he be the person to introduce financing for hospitalization in the country? The idea seemed just too radical, but wasn't that true of many ideas that became booming success stories? Looking at the success of Facebook, Google, Uber, Ola Cabs, Oyo Rooms and all those similar companies that had created an entirely new business out of nothing, perhaps the idea wasn't so unrealistic, after all!

Now, before we proceed, it is important to understand Tushar's background. He was a management graduate as well as a CFA—or a chartered financial analyst. In other words, he clearly understood finance and financing. Further, he had spent over four years in managing a 'healthcare' fund that invested across companies in the healthcare sector. Interestingly, the investors in this fund were all doctors. And, therefore, Tushar brought to the table an understanding of both healthcare as well as finance—quite a rare combination, you would agree, and just the right mix for the venture he was thinking of.

And so Tushar put on his thinking cap and began to work out the contours of his brand-new business. Most importantly, he realized that he needed a co-founder, and he found just the right person—Soumya Arora—who had worked with Oyo Rooms and was therefore quite familiar with operations. And together the two young friends launched Uno Finance—an interesting name and in keeping with the ambitions of its founders.

Tushar realized that lending was a highly regulated business, restricted to banks and NBFCs (non-banking finance companies). And the regulator was the RBI, which issued licences to these two categories to lend money. The RBI had laid out certain conditions for any company to qualify as an NBFC, and one of these conditions was the amount of capital the company needed to have. After all, it could not lend money till it had enough money in the first place, could it? Based on these conditions, the RBI would issue the company a licence. In a nutshell, therefore, if you wanted to be in the lending business, you had to get a licence from the RBI, and to get the licence you had to satisfy certain conditions, such as the amount of capital you had to have. Period.

Tushar realized that getting a licence at this early stage was not going to be easy, so he decided on the next best option. He tied up with an NBFC, which was in the financing space anyway, and became a kind of front end to them. Essentially, he would bring in the customer, he would do the due diligence to ensure that it was a genuine customer, who was likely to pay back the loan, and then make this customer available to the NBFC to fund. A simple partnership, for which Uno Finance would take a commission from the NBFC.

The next step, of course, was to tie up with hospitals. And here Tushar's background in the healthcare space came in handy. He had realized by then that patients would select the best hospital that they could afford—assuming, of course, other factors such as proximity to their home were taken care of. And this was the killer. Because of the lack of health insurance, or in some cases insufficient health insurance, many patients were forced to knock off the more expensive hospitals—and possible the better ones. Conversely, most hospitals lost out on several potential patients, simply because these patients could not afford their charges. And the million-dollar question was: Could Tushar's EMI-based model make these hospitals more affordable, and therefore increase their occupancy?

Tushar was right. This was indeed a problem, and hospitals were, in fact, very keen on the idea. 'Sure,' most of them said, 'if you can give the patient an EMI option, we'd be happy to share a commission with you.' And as hospitals began to sign up, Tushar and Soumya began to get more and more excited. The venture was actually taking off.

Of course, it was also important to figure out how to reach the customer—the poor chap who was actually going to be hospitalized, or whose relative was going to be hospitalized! After all, wasn't this the reason for setting up the business in the first place? Now, the founders had realized early on that it was pointless doing advertising—even focused digital advertising. Because most customers simply did not see themselves as being in a situation where they might need hospitalization. The right time to catch the customer was when he or she actually visited a hospital to initiate the admissions process. And, therefore, the obvious solution was to have a kiosk or counter at the hospital entrance, manned by one of Uno's employees. The patient would walk in, hopefully notice the kiosk and the financing option, and that's when the sales process would begin.

And that is how Uno Finance started. Interestingly, personal loans were fairly commonly available at this stage and usually required details of the loanee, such as his income tax returns, salary slips and bank statements. Based on these, his ability to pay back the loan was assessed. But, of course, there was the other question—the intention to pay it back. Haven't you seen enough super-rich people simply floating on money but refusing to pay back their loans? That's right, Uno would need to check out *not only the ability of the loanee to pay back the loan, but also his intention to pay it back.* No more Nirav Modis and Mehul Choksis, please! For which the company would check out the payment history of past loans or credit cards that the individual had taken—typically through his or her CIBIL score. And once these two were checked out, well, the loan could be approved.

Of course, there were two important caveats. First of all, hospitalization was always risky business. What if—unfortunately—

the patient did not survive? Or what if he or she did survive but could not resume their regular job? How would they pay back the loan? That was a major, major problem, wasn't it? And therefore, our young founders often gave the loan not to the patient but to a family member. By the same logic, they would check the income, bank statements, etc., as well as the intention to pay *of the family member*, rather than of the patient.

Secondly, processing of loans might take a week or even more—at least in the case of banks. Now you might be willing to wait for a week to buy, say a car, but would you be willing to wait for a week to get admitted into a hospital? Wouldn't hospitalization usually need immediate admission and therefore no delay in the start of your treatment? You see? Even if banks were willing to give out loans in such cases, they would be too slow. Fortunately, several NBFCs that operated online had worked out risk-assessment models, where they approved loans within a matter of hours or, at best, a day. The checking would be less thorough, and therefore the risks of default would be higher. But guess what—these NBFCs charged significantly higher interest to make up for the higher risk. And this is what the founders of Uno Finance did. They charged somewhat higher interest rates, approved loans fast (or rejected them), and everyone was happy.

And now we must share something really interesting with you. One morning while shaving (yes, while shaving), Tushar had a brainwave. And in his excitement, he cut himself. However, that is not the point. The point is: What if they were to charge no interest at all from the patient? For instance, suppose a patient had to be admitted for a procedure that would cost a total of Rs 1.2 lakh. Uno would then ask him to pay the loan back in six monthly EMIs of Rs 20,000 per month. In other words, *the patient would simply be paying the original hospital charges without any additional interest* (unless, of course, he defaulted, which is a different issue). Can you imagine any patient in his right mind refusing this option? No interest to be paid on the principal? And that's exactly what happened. Patients simply lapped up this instalment plan, and Uno Finance began to grow rapidly.

But hang on, you might be saying. That's silly. If they didn't charge interest, how did Uno make any money at all? And by extension, how did the NBFC that actually lent the funds make money?

Aha. They did make money. Because hospitals were quite impressed with the idea. They figured that they would get several patients who might have otherwise found their hospital unaffordable. So they were willing to give Uno enough of a commission for each patient. That commission, ladies and gentlemen, was sufficient to cover the interest that the NBFC wanted, with enough left over for each transaction to be profitable for Uno Finance. In other words, the unit economics of the business was positive.

Happily, the concept caught on. Yes, there was some competition, but it was a very, very nascent industry and the opportunity was large. Hospitals realized that they could get a completely new segment of patients—those who could not otherwise afford treatment there— and were quite willing to sign up. And, of course, patients—who were surprised at the zero-interest loan option, lapped it up. Interestingly, there was also a segment of patients who took pride in the brand of hospital they had been to. Just imagine the following conversation:

Friend 1: '*Yaar, suna tune operation karaaya hai* [I heard that you've had an operation].'

Friend 2: '*Haan, par ab theek hoon* [Yes, but I'm okay now].'

Friend 1: '*Kaun sa hospital tha* [Which hospital was it]?'

Friend 2 (said with a certain quiet pride): 'Max.'

Friend 1: '*Woh toh bahut mehenga hoga* [That must be very expensive].'

Friend 2 (nonchalantly): '*Haan, par paise ki koi chinta nahin thi* (Yes, but money was not an issue].'

Friend 1 (seething): 'Oh?'

So you can see the kind of impact Uno Finance had on the social standing of the patient! Now that they could afford the brand, they happily got their treatment from these elite hospitals, which led to further business for these hospitals. And, therefore, Uno Finance began to grow. But then the inevitable happened. They ran short of money. And so . . .

The Pitch and After

Dear reader, what do you think the angels did? Obvious, isn't it? They lapped up the story and our young founders were able to get funding fairly easily. The investors realized that this was a very large and, for all practical purposes, untapped business opportunity. Sure, there were other players in personal finance, but this was a new target segment—one where the spending was absolutely essential—and that was enough for them.

At this stage, it is interesting to hear Tushar on the subject of funding:

We realized that fundraising in the Indian and Western environments are significantly different. In the West, where the ecosystem has matured over time, you can get funding even to build your product. However, in India, that's not easy. Most investors first want to see at least a minimum viable product, or MVP, before they are willing to invest. Which means that to build this MVP, you need to use your own money, or, at best, money from your family and friends. And that's exactly what we did.

Now for the next step in the journey of our two friends. As we have been saying over and over again in this book, entry barriers are extremely critical to any business. Uno Finance had started providing finance in an area that not too many NBFCs had tapped thus far, but was that enough? Once this area was seen to be a large opportunity, what was to prevent other guys—especially the big ones—from entering it? And therefore wiping out smaller players like Uno?

Fortunately, our founders were smart. They had realized early on that this would not be their ultimate business model—that had to be different. And they had it all planned out. As mentioned earlier on, hospitalization is a risky business. Unfortunately, in the worst case, it could end up in the patient not surviving. Or possibly not being able to work for an extended period of time, and therefore not having the money to pay back his or her loan. And therefore the loans that were not paid back—which we call NPAs, or non-performing assets—could potentially be very high. So in the current business model, only a fraction of the loan applications were approved. For instance, if the patient was the only breadwinner in the family and his current bank balance and assets such as fixed deposits and mutual funds were not too high, the risk of him or her being unable to pay back the loan was high. And, therefore, the loan was unlikely to be sanctioned. The key issue was that—for reasons of risk—*only a fraction of the loan applications could be approved*. And this, by the way, was what competitors were also doing.

But what if the patient were a young man who had damaged the ligaments in his knee while playing football and therefore needed knee surgery? Obviously there was no risk of non-survival in this kind of surgery. Further, the risk of not getting back to work was again zero—at worst he might need to use crutches for some time. In other words—and this is the crucial bit—*from a lender's point of view, the medical risk in this case was virtually zero*. And, therefore, there was no problem in granting a loan to him.

You see? In the earlier business model, Uno Finance would knock out a large number of applicants and not grant them a loan, just as their competitors would. But what if they were to look at the details of the case—such as the exact medical problem, the procedure the patient would have to undergo and the associated risk? And how well equipped the hospital was for this particular procedure? And how competent the doctor was to perform the operation? Wouldn't that give Uno Finance a far better idea of the risk involved? Based on this more accurate assessment of risk, Uno Finance could actually grant a loan to many, many more patients, and therefore address a segment of the market that its competitors could not. Brilliant, wasn't it?

By the way, if you think this was a trivial example, you are right. But what if the patient were admitted with, say, inflammation of the oesophagus? Or an oro-antral fistula, which required the Caldwell-Luc procedure? Or any of the myriad medical conditions that required hospitalization? (By the way, we're sure you don't understand these terms. Neither do we, for that matter. But these are genuine medical conditions and procedures.) We and you, dear reader, would have no idea of the risks associated with these surgeries. It would require doctors—no, specialists—to decide the level of risk. Even that might not be enough, and you would probably need to go through papers in medical journals that focused on this particular condition and the treatment involved. So you would need several specialist doctors, who would need to continuously browse through medical journals. And use the research-based data presented there to figure out risk levels for each kind of treatment. And that, ladies and gentlemen, is exactly what Uno Finance did.

So, while in the first phase they had played safe and only given loans where the risk was obviously low, in the second phase they would use the data they had gathered to analyse these medical parameters and then take a decision on the loan. And that, ladies and gentlemen, was their unique offering. Or shall we say, their entry barrier!

Clearly, the second phase required additional funding—to build the analytics capability based on medical data, as well as to grow rapidly. And so our two young friends went off in search of investors once again. As you might expect, the investors were very positive. This seemed to be a unique business, even more so in the second phase. Potentially a huge market and virtually untapped. Further, the founders had successfully tied up with several hospitals and shown terrific growth. In fact, at the time of writing this book, they were operating across more than 300 hospitals in the NCR and serving more than 1,000 patients on a monthly basis. So guess what? Our founders were able to raise three times the earlier round, and at a valuation that was more than twice that in the earlier round. And the future looks rosier than ever.

To end this story, we hope you and your family never need to be hospitalized. Even if you do, we do hope money is not an issue. But if it is, you now know that you do not need to dip into your savings.

Because you now have Uno Finance . . .

Analysis

So that's the highly promising story of Uno Finance, which has successfully raised two rounds of funding. Interestingly, the business ticked virtually all boxes of our PERSISTENT framework. A highly INNOVATIVE solution to a PROBLEM simply waiting to be solved, through the use of analytics based on medical research. Potentially a huge MARKET SIZE. And an ENTRY BARRIER that built up in the second phase as it started using medical data for risk assessment. And this ENTRY BARRIER will only grow with time, as the company gathers more and more data on Indian patients and uses it to fine-tune its risk assessment.

Was there a RISK to the business? In the first phase, yes, since any NBFC could enter the business. But the second phase obviously reduced this RISK.

And, of course, it was a TEAM with just the right background—finance, healthcare and technology. A great cocktail for a bright future. So let's wish the company and its founders the very best . . .

The Impact of the Coronavirus—or Any Other Crisis

You must have guessed this one by now. COVID-19 has made health a very high priority for everyone. And if you need to be hospitalized, you would want a really good hospital—which Uno Finance has now made possible. So for Tushar and his company, the future is bright. And for you, dear reader, remember, if your start-up has anything to do with health, it's likely to do well in today's environment. And investors might just flock to you . . .

Finally, check out our PERSISTENT table on the next page:

The PERSISTENT Approach Applied to Uno Finance

	Issue	Uno Finance
P	**PROBLEM:** Are you solving a real problem? Will people pay?	Problem of affordability of the right treatment and hospital.
E	**EARNINGS MODEL**	Commission from the hospital for each transaction. Unit economics positive.
R	**RISKS** and how you will mitigate them	Risk of competition coming in. Reduced in the second phase.
S	**SIZE OF THE MARKET**	Very large.
I	**INNOVATION**	The use of analytics based on medical research to assess risk and therefore sanction loans.
S	**SCALABILITY**	Highly scalable.
T	**TEAM**, starting with the founders	The founders had the right background of management, finance, healthcare and technology.
E	**ENTRY BARRIERS**	A large database of health-related statistics, collected from medical journals.
N	**NICHE:** When the market is crowded, identify a niche	Launching healthcare-focused financing products—which is a huge NICHE.
T	**TRACTION**	Operating across more than 300 hospitals across the NCR. Serving more than 1,000 patients on a monthly basis.

Let's Meet Pradeep Gupta, Founder and Chairman, CyberMedia; Co-Founder, Indian Angel Network

As most of you are aware, Pradeep Gupta—popularly known as PG—is the iconic founder and chief of CyberMedia, the publishers of leading computer magazines such as *Dataquest* and *PCQuest*. He is also one of the co-founders of Indian Angel Network, and a prolific angel investor himself. Now PG has been an old friend and mentor to both of us for many years. Quite naturally, therefore, when we started this book, the first person we went to for his views on start-ups was our good friend PG. So let's hear him out:

> There are two broad approaches to building your business. One is to bootstrap and grow profitably, even if it is not too rapidly. Obviously you would delay funding, in that case. The other one is to raise lots of funding and grow rapidly. And one of the most common questions I am asked is, 'Which option should we choose?'
>
> You see, if you have an easily replicable business—one where there isn't any great entry barrier—you must grow fast.

157

Because size and brand are then your only entry barriers. Otherwise someone with more money will overtake you. On the other hand, if you are building something unique— which would usually be technology-based—your entry barrier is the IP, and not necessarily the size of the business. In such a case, you should bootstrap as long as you can. Of course, keep your concept under wraps. Incidentally, being part of an incubator is a great idea for such start-ups. Because that cuts down your costs—and perhaps also gets you some grants. And most important, you also get mentoring. Build a solid core, check out a proof of concept and then look for funding.

As an investor, what do I look for in a founder? Well, first of all, passion. Creating a business is a lifetime's commitment and you cannot do it without passion. You must also have a vision for your business. And, of course, the ability to take risks. By the way, these are the qualities that set entrepreneurs apart from salaried CEOs. And yes, if there are multiple founders, they must have complementary skills. So if one of them is a smart techie, the other must understand business.

And what puts me off? That's easy. Smooth-talkers, smart alecs, braggers without substance. Poor listeners are also a no-no. And most of all, entrepreneurs who try to fool the investor. My advice to all young men and women reading this book is to please be genuine. Else the investor will see through you.

And finally, two important lessons. Who you get money from is important. What should the start-up look for in the investor? There must be an alignment of thought between the investor and the entrepreneur, and there must be value-add from the investor—not just the money. Lastly, don't worry too much about valuations. Most investors are reasonable people, and they know that this is a partnership, not a one-sided arrangement. They realize that you need to have skin in the game. Of course, if you meet an investor who doesn't, well, he's probably not the right investor for you.

So those were the wise words from our friend PG. Thanks as always, PG. And we'll get back to you for our next book.

15

QACCO and Their Unique Holiday Resorts

Have you ever been to a cute little resort called Sherlock? If not, you MUST go there. It's about five kilometres outside Ooty, and its claim to fame is its association with one of greatest fictional characters ever. Yes, you've guessed right—it's a theme-based hotel, and the theme is built around stories of the famous detective Sherlock Holmes. So it has statues of Sherlock Holmes, photographs from the TV series, even the menu is based on his stories. And, above all, the rooms are named after his stories. So you have a room called 'The Baskervilles', another called 'Gloria Scott', a third one called . . .

But you get the drift, don't you? A hotel—actually a small resort—modelled on the adventures of the great detective. And for fans like us, staying there was a terrific experience, as you can imagine. We actually felt we were living the Sherlock Holmes stories!

Okay, let's take you to another resort. This one is called 'Cloud's End', a few kilometres outside Mussoorie, in the hills of Uttarakhand. And it is literally at the end of the clouds. It's in the middle of nowhere—but from there you get a magnificent view of the snow-clad mountains in the upper reaches of the state. Interestingly, the owner of this resort—one Mr Agarwal—does not have an electricity connection. At least he didn't when I (Dhruv) had been there. They do have a generator but that is only switched on in the evenings and mornings. Even the road leading up to his resort is 'kutcha', or unpaved. Why? Agarwal sahib is very clear about the kind of guests he wants. They must be nature lovers, and he is committed to providing them a unique experience, as close to nature as they can imagine. So he will sit with his guests in the evening and regale them with stories and folklore about the mountains, the jungles and the villages. The highlight of the stay, of course, is that you might be able to spot a leopard. We had once asked Mr Agarwal what we should do in case we saw a leopard, and his reply was candid. 'If you see a leopard, you need to do nothing. Whatever has to be done, the leopard will do . . .'

Anyhow, let's leave the fascinating subject of what the leopard will do, and ask a very basic question, 'What is common between these two resorts—or hotels?' That's right, these are not conventional hotels. They are what we would call boutique hotels—smaller than conventional hotels, often theme-based, and usually very different. Each of them offers a unique experience to the traveller, unlike the Taj Hotels and Sheratons of the world. And, most of all, they do not appear on typical travel sites such as MakeMyTrip or Yatra. Or if they do, they are probably tucked away right at the bottom of the search results and therefore never get noticed.

How terrible! Such great places to stay, and they are not even noticed. Isn't that sad? Dear reader, if you think so, we must compliment you. Because your thinking is very similar to that of Chaitanya Jha and Abhinav Imandi, two bright young MBAs from the Management Development Institute in Gurgaon. And, we may add, former students of mine (Dhruv). These two classmates were smart, and they smelt a business opportunity here. Why not create an online travel portal catering exclusively to such boutique hotels and the kinds of travellers they would attract?

And that's how the idea behind QACCO took shape. As you might imagine, QACCO was short for 'Quality Accommodation', and it was solely focused on boutique hotels and resorts. The young friends realized that there was a large population out there that did not want to stay in conventional hotels. They wanted something different. At the same time, hotels and resorts that did offer something different were hard to find. Enter QACCO—which brought these boutique hotels face to face with customers who would love them.

Now these two classmates realized quite rightly that being a travel intermediary was a very tough business. Customers might use QACCO to discover a hotel that was of interest to them, but then search on the Internet to figure out where they would get the maximum discount on this hotel. Sadly, therefore, QACCO might make boutique hotels discoverable but the business would go elsewhere. Signing exclusive contracts with these hotels was a way out, but then the hotel owner would demand a guarantee on the occupancy QACCO would provide—which they obviously could not commit to. After a lot of thinking, alternately over beer and coffee (with the beer providing the stimulus to the grey cells, naturally), the founders realized that the name of the game was discounting. They simply had to offer their customers the lowest price for these hotels—lower than any other intermediary such as MakeMyTrip or Yatra. That was the only way they could get customers to make their bookings through QACCO.

And, at the same time, they had to be viable. Which, of course, meant positive unit economics.

Tough one, wasn't it? Give a larger discount than anyone else and still run a viable business? However, as we've already mentioned, our founders were smart. After all, they had studied under me (Dhruv), hadn't they ☺? So they started meeting owners of these hotels and made an interesting proposition to them. Let's look at a typical conversation between the QACCO founders and a hotel owner. We'll dispense with the inessentials such as 'good morning', 'would you like a cup of tea?', etc. After all, we don't want to waste your time, do we? So here goes:

QACCO founders: 'Sir, we searched for your hotel on several travel sites, but in many cases it didn't come up. Or even if it did, it was very low down in the search results and therefore didn't get noticed.'

Hotel owner (disinterested): 'Unfortunately, that is true. I would like my hotel to get noticed because it's actually a very unique place. But I don't want to spend on ads. Too expensive.'

QACCO founders: 'Sir, we have a database of interested travellers who have registered on our site. These travellers have signed up with us and we regularly send them mails about possible holiday stays. And we could include your hotel in these mails, and thereby popularize it.'

Hotel owner (looking less bored): 'Oh? Interesting.'

QACCO founders: 'And sir, we can take it a step forward. Since you have a seaside hotel, travellers would typically do things like snorkelling, scuba diving or even a peaceful boat ride through the backwaters. Many travellers would perhaps end up at your hotel and book these options directly with the operators of these activities, so you do not get any revenue from these activities. But we can offer our registered users full packages rather than just a hotel stay. And we would source these packages through you—so you actually get a share in the boat ride or the snorkelling.'

Hotel owner (fully awake now and ordering filter coffee for everyone): 'That's a good idea.'

QACCO founders (now closing in for the kill): 'As you can see, sir, your occupancy would probably go up, and so would the revenue per transaction. You are no longer booking only room nights. All we ask, sir, is that you give us a higher discount than you would give to any other travel intermediary.'

Hotel owner (after due deliberation, and lots of back and forth with his business instincts): 'Fine. Let's go ahead. I'll give you 3 per cent more than the others. But no more. And no exclusivity!'

Elated QACCO founders: 'Thank you, sir. And that filter coffee was great!'

Dear reader, cut out the masala in the above conversation, and you can see what the QACCO founders achieved. Higher discounts. Which they could then pass on to their customers.

But hang on. We haven't finished yet. There is more, so keep reading. Chaitanya and Abhinav realized that, like all start-ups, they did not have money to market the concept. So they decided on a highly focused method called B2B2C marketing. Now we're sure you understand this term, but for someone who doesn't, what it means is this: QACCO was a business, so that's the first B. They wanted to contact travellers, or, in other words, consumers. So that's the C. And they did it through the employers of these consumers, which was the B in the middle. In other words, they used 'Business to Business to Consumer' marketing, or B2B2C for short. An ingenious method and very popular with a lot of marketers now.

How did it work? Quite simple. Every organization has an HR department, and one of their jobs is to keep their employees motivated and happy so they stay on. A common way to do this is to have an employee benefits programme. QACCO started meeting HR heads of organizations and positioned their offering as a benefit to their employees. As an example, if Tata Motors were to tie up with QACCO, their employees would be entitled to all the discounted holiday offers from QACCO. The organization had to pay nothing. All they had to do was send a mail to all their employees informing them about the QACCO scheme. Alternatively, they could put it up on the company intranet. Interested employees would then register with QACCO and get the appropriate mailers. No cost and no effort for the organization.

As you can imagine, organizations were happy with the concept, and within a couple of months four of them had signed up. QACCO had successfully implemented the low-cost B2B2C marketing model.

But that's still not all. When our founders went to subsequent hotels, they had an additional benefit to tom-tom. 'Sir, we can now guarantee you an exclusive clientele. These will all be middle- to senior-level corporate executives.' The hotel owners were obviously happy, and the discounting continued—even increased, in some cases. In fact, we checked out their rates, and, yes, for the kinds of hotels QACCO catered to, they did offer the lowest rates in most cases.

And so QACCO moved forward. A great concept, low-cost marketing, in fact, a win-win for everyone—for travellers, for hotels, for employers and for QACCO itself. Hotel sign-ups increased, registered users began to increase and, as a consequence, room nights also went up. Things were looking good. In fact, the founders also realized the concept could easily be extended to homestays—just like Airbnb. Which would give them huge scalability. Yes sir, things were definitely looking up. And this was just the right time to raise funds.

And so they inevitably found themselves at the doors of the angels . . .

The Pitch

As you can imagine, the presentation went very well. An interesting niche, with the potential to expand into the huge homestay market. The angels liked the low-cost marketing model and the innovative approach of creating holiday packages, rather than simply selling room nights. Admittedly there were competitors lurking around, such as HolidayIQ in the online space and DPauls in the offline as well as online space, but the angels figured that any good opportunity would probably have competitors anyway. They also liked the fact that the founders had been able to get good terms from hotels. Potentially, the company could even expand into foreign travel. And, above all, these were two experienced people from one of the premier business schools in the country. What more could an investor ask for?

Of course, there were a few niggling worries. For one thing, it was a known fact that the travel intermediary space had no real entry barriers. And then there was also the seasonality factor—most families would take their holidays during the summer or the winter season—when schools were shut. Very few holidays during the monsoons or exam time. But then travel was known to be a seasonal business, and you had to accept that. Finally, of course, if QACCO did not expand successfully into homestays, the market for boutique hotels might not be too large. As a consequence of these negatives, some investors stayed away. But there were others who felt this was a good opportunity and decided to put in their hard-earned money into the business. Interestingly, the founders were able to raise a total of almost a crore from two angel networks.

Yes, our young friends were able to raise money, and there was tremendous learning in the process. This is what Chaitanya had to say:

> Raising funds can take time. You need to be mentally prepared for being actively involved in these discussions for a six-to-nine-month period, till the money hits the bank. In fact, I would go so far as to say that raising funds is almost a full-time job. It distracts you from running your business. We were fortunate that we had two founders, and so one of us took on this responsibility while the other focused entirely on the business.
>
> Also, it is crucial to be absolutely transparent with your investors. In the middle of raising our round of funding, our then CTO left for a personal project in Australia, leaving us hanging. We reached out to each investor and explained the situation to them. We were transparent with them and told them that we would be hiring a full-time senior developer after closing the round. They appreciated our honesty and did not back out of their investments.
>
> Remember, always build a strong proof of concept before you start looking for funding—essentially an MVP, or a minimum viable product. The very nature of conversation would change from 'Is your idea just a thought in the sky?' to 'Okay, how do you scale things from here?'. This will also

give you, as the entrepreneur, a tonne of confidence before you meet potential investors.

Finally, having got through the bootstrapping grind, you would have learnt to use the investors' money wisely. And remember, before you have raised funds, you can still pace your experiments as per your own speed. After raising funds, you are always on the clock. Our advice to you, therefore, is: Bootstrap as long as you can before raising money.

After the Funding

Flush with funds, our two young friends went into growth mode. The money was used to hunt for additional hotels to sign up with, and to get more and more employers on board. Some of it, of course, went into development and fine-tuning their website, so as to continuously enhance the user experience. They even experimented with off-sites—conferences organized by corporates at interesting destinations—although they realized that this was not really a scalable business. On the whole, however, growth was good and the founders were happy . . .

However, happy times do not always last. One day, the two young founders got together for a serious discussion. 'We seem to be reaching some kind of saturation—there aren't that many boutique hotels, and we've already signed up with a large number of them. So how do we continue to grow?'

Dear reader, as you are aware, small start-ups that have raised funds cannot afford to stagnate. After all, they do have a commitment to provide an exit to their investors, and that, too, at a higher valuation. And that was the concern our two founders had. To overcome this problem, they decided to get into conventional hotels—which were obviously far, far larger in number. But wait. The benefit they had with boutique hotels was not valid any more when it came to these regular hotels. They simply could not get the kind of discounts the larger players got.

Our founders were persistent, though. They realized that this was a volume game. You provided volumes to hotels, and you got discounts. So they needed to become a 'volume' player. Perhaps by getting a strategic investor with deep pockets on board—someone who might be interested in getting into this space. And so our young, tireless founders started approaching possible suitors. Unfortunately, it didn't work. Because booking packages with boutique hotels was not a large enough business to interest the big guys. And they had no background in conventional hotels.

And so our friends had to wind up the company. Sadder, but much, much wiser. They realized that one of the key things any business needed was a large enough market size. Enough to interest both VCs and strategic investors. Further, to compete effectively, they needed some kind of entry barrier. And discounting—no matter how they managed it—was not an effective enough entry barrier. Because a large player wanting to grab their market share could easily offer higher discounts.

Yes, the company did close down. However, there is no reason for you to feel sorry for them. These two young men are bright and extremely hard-working, and had learnt a lot from this venture. They are both doing very well right now, and are far, far wiser after QACCO. At some stage we're sure they will get back to creating a new start-up. And with the learning they have had, they are bound to be successful.

We would definitely be investing in their next start-up. Wouldn't you?

Analysis

And that, ladies and gentlemen, was QACCO. It was definitely solving the PROBLEM faced by boutique hotels—namely the fact that they were usually not noticed in the huge mass of hotels. It also increased the revenues for these hotels by selling packages as against just room nights. And, of course, it ensured a certain kind of clientele—middle- to senior-level corporate executives, which is what all hotels want. On the other hand, with the consumer—or the traveller—it was more of an opportunity than a problem. There were many travellers who wanted unique experiences and QACCO provided these. An interesting NICHE in the otherwise very crowded travel-portal market. Driven by a qualified, experienced and passionate TEAM of founders.

Unfortunately, where they got hit was in the SIZE OF THE MARKET. Because there simply were not enough boutique hotels going around. It wasn't a large enough NICHE. And once they attempted to pivot the business model by getting into conventional hotels, well, they had no ENTRY BARRIER. And, therefore, they could not compete with the biggies in the game. And that was the RISK with the business, which ultimately pulled them down.

Let's, however, end on a positive note. We have mentioned all along that in the early stages of a business, most investors look at the TEAM, or the entrepreneur, even more than the business. And these were undoubtedly terrific entrepreneurs. With the experience they had gathered, they are bound to do well in future.

Finally, let's share a secret with you. Only for you—please don't broadcast it. We have already kept aside money to put into their next venture, whenever that happens . . .

The Impact of the Coronavirus—or Any Other Crisis

Surely you are aware of the answer by now! The COVID-19 crisis has had a significant negative impact on all kinds of travel and tourism. Therefore, industries such as hotels and airlines are likely to take a hit. Obviously, investors are shying away from such sectors as well. So avoid getting into these spaces—there are lots and lots of other areas that have benefited from the crisis. Why not look at them instead?

Finally, what does our table look like? Here it is:

The PERSISTENT Approach Applied to QACCO

	Issue	QACCO
P	**PROBLEM:** Are you solving a real problem? Will people pay?	For boutique hotels, they were definitely solving the problem of being noticed, as well as helping to increase their revenues through holiday packages.
E	**EARNINGS MODEL**	Margin on each transaction. Unit economics positive.
R	**RISKS** and how you will mitigate them	The possibility of large competitors getting into the same space—which actually happened.
S	**SIZE OF THE MARKET**	Not large enough.
I	**INNOVATION**	B2B2C marketing to cut costs.
S	**SCALABILITY**	Moderate. Manual intervention required for each transaction.
T	**TEAM**, starting with the founders	Founders highly qualified, dedicated and passionate about the concept.
E	**ENTRY BARRIERS**	None. Discounting can never be a long-term entry barrier.
N	**NICHE:** When the market is crowded, identify a niche	Boutique hotels, within the extremely crowded space of online travel intermediaries.
T	**TRACTION**	Partnerships with four corporates and fifty boutique hotels. Some successful transactions at the time of applying for funding.

Let's Meet Sairee Chahal,
Founder and CEO, SHEROES

Which is the clear market leader in building communities for women? That's right—it's Sheroes.com, started by the young, ebullient Sairee Chahal. Whose motto is very simple, 'When women come to SHEROES, they benefit from it.' When we spoke to Sairee, she was more than willing to share her views on start-ups and funding. Let's hear what she had to say:

> Every entrepreneur must ask herself the question, 'Do I really need funding?' Some businesses can be successful without funding. However, funding gives you the ability to experiment, make mistakes, fail, learn and then retry. You cannot do this if you do not have money to back you up. Also, tech products are expensive to build, and for this you need funding anyway. But please don't build a company for funding. Build a real business. Don't play the valuation game—in any case, valuations autocorrect over time.
>
> What do investors look for in start-ups? First of all, it's sincerity and conviction about their venture. Which, naturally, includes their depth of understanding of the business. And, of

course, openness—no one wants to invest in a company where the founders have fixed ideas. In case there are co-founders, they should ideally bring in complementary skills. And finally, entrepreneurs who are focused on their business. Those with the attitude, 'Funding or no funding, we'll go ahead with our business.' And just to add an interesting bit of experience, 'Funding is given to people who don't really need it—not to those who are desperate.'

And now, what should the entrepreneur look for in investors? That's right, it is very, very important to get the right investors. First of all, please avoid catching investors who are looking for a quick exit. That puts unnecessary pressure on your business. I have found it great to take money from successful entrepreneurs, who are willing to wait it out. Also, try and get people who are familiar with your industry. That helps to get advice, and since these people understand the space, they will not make unreasonable demands. Above all, take money from people who you respect and who can add value.

Finally, remember, when you need money is not when you start chasing it. That's too late. Start planning well in advance and do your homework. Importantly, hang out with investors and understand their thinking. Figure out what they are looking for and what you are looking for in them. Over time it will be far easier to get money from them. And, of course, it will be a win-win.

And if you can do all this, well, your chances of getting funding from the right investors are that much brighter. I hope you do get that funding. Wish you all the best.

Thanks, Sairee. That's truly great advice. And we're sure young entrepreneurs reading this book will benefit from it. Thanks once again.

Section IV

So What Should You Do?

16

The Investment Process

Dear reader, you've heard lots of stories so far. Stories about start-ups that managed to get funding and those who didn't. You've seen pitch sessions, you've seen what angels look for and how they react. You've also seen how VCs react in later stages of funding. But what you haven't seen is the actual process. How did these start-ups reach investors in the first place? Did the investors come to the pitch sessions with their chequebooks, all ready to write out their cheques over the coffee that followed? If not, what were the steps after the pitch session? When was the shareholder agreement drafted? How was the valuation arrived at? Etc., etc., etc. . . .

Yes sir, raising money is not so simple. You would typically go through a multistep process before those mouth-watering cheques are actually in your pocket. And this chapter talks about all these steps. So let's start at very beginning (a very good place to start, as Julie Andrews had said in the movie *The Sound of Music*). And since your first port of call will be angel networks, let's first understand what these are, and how they work.

Angel Networks

We've briefly seen angel networks in Chapter 2, but now let's examine them in some detail. In the early part of this century, there were very few angels in existence. Most of them were super-rich businessmen and extremely hard to track down. Contacting one of them was a major achievement in itself. Fortunately, that has now changed. Today we have several thousands of angel investors in the country. How did this happen? Well, as you would agree, 'start-up' has become a magic word today. No party is complete without a discussion on the merits of Amazon vs Flipkart, or Ola Cabs vs Uber, or how Naukri and MakeMyTrip have captured their respective markets, or the phenomenal funding that Paytm got from the Chinese giant Alibaba and, more recently, from the famous investor Warren Buffet, or . . .

But you get the idea, don't you? Start-ups are among the hottest topics that can be discussed over a peg of Black Label whisky today. And even hotter are the phenomenal valuations they command. Flipkart, Ola Cabs, Byju's and Oyo Rooms are all unicorns—in other words, they have raised funding at a valuation of over a billion dollars. And many more unicorns are being born every year. Then, of course, there are the soonicorns—or those that are about to break into the club soon. And yes, the babycorns ☺. The pink, white, green and purple papers—not to mention the TV channels—go berserk with the latest success stories. So who in their right mind would not want to own a slice of this disruptive story in India? And that explains the significant increase in the number of angel investors.

Now here's the interesting part. Let's say a start-up needs a crore in funding. In the good old days we had very few angels. Each angel would then have had to shell out a large amount—typically Rs 25 lakh or more—so that three or four angels could raise the figure among themselves. But with the number of angels mushrooming, and lots of angels willing to put in money, the amount per angel could be as little as Rs 5 lakh. That's right. Just Rs 5 lakh. And fifteen to twenty angels between them can now raise the crore required.

Aha! We knew you'd get it. To put Rs 5 lakh into a start-up, you do not need to be a super-rich businessman. And you definitely do not need to have the good fortune of having been born into one of our erstwhile royal families. You could be a senior salaried professional— or even a retired one. You could be a chartered accountant or a lawyer. You could even be a professor, like me (Dhruv). And what do we call such angels? 'Aam aadmi angels', naturally!

If you recall from Chapter 2, angel investors hunt in packs— rather like wolves. And the reason for this should now be clear to you. You see, an aam aadmi angel investor rarely invests more than Rs 5–10 lakh in any start-up. And therefore lots of such angels are required to raise any meaningful figure such as a crore or even half a crore. Now it is obviously impossible for any start-up to approach so many investors individually, let alone locating them in the first place. Which is why we have angel networks, each having a few hundred angels as members. And so the start-up only needs to be in touch with the network, and not each individual angel.

There is another reason for these networks. Rich angels—also called super angels—would usually have an army of people at their beck and call. People such as business analysts, chartered accountants and lawyers to analyse the business of the start-up, do the appropriate due diligence and, of course, draft their agreements. But what about the poor aam aadmi angel? He is on his own and needs support. Who provides this support? Very simply, the angel network. So the network evaluates each start-up and then shortlists the ones that seem the most promising. The founders are then asked to make a presentation or pitch. After the pitch session, start-ups that investors are interested in are evaluated in further detail (unfortunately, the others go home with coffee and cookies). Finally, those that are ripe for investment are given a term sheet. Which is rather like an MoU. Essentially similar to the final shareholder agreement that will be signed but without the details (see Chapter 20). By the way, this is also the stage at which the angels make their commitment to invest in the company, although the actual money is put in once the shareholder agreement is signed.

But hang on. Even this is not the end. The start-up has only been through a business and technical evaluation so far. It now needs to go through a thorough due diligence process, which includes accounting, statutory compliances and legal issues. And if it comes out unscathed from there, the shareholder agreement between the company and the potential investors is drafted out. And then the best part—the cheques are issued, which the founder gratefully grabs. By the way, mentoring by the investors already began when the investors took their decision to invest.

Notice that it's a fairly long process with multiple experts involved at every stage. Can the aam aadmi angel possibly go through this process on his own? Of course not. He needs help. And, ladies and gentlemen, that help is provided by the angel network. For a small fee to cover the cost of the transaction. So that's why we have angel networks, and that's why founders need to approach them.

Contacting Angel Networks

Having explained the process that angel networks go through, let's see how the various friends we have met contacted them. Starting with our young friend Abhishek Barari of MyCuteOffice fame. Abhishek was attending a boot camp conceptualized by the well-known organization TiE (The Indus Entrepreneurs). As part of this camp, he got to meet several angel investors. One of them was interested in his somewhat unique concept and asked him to make a pitch. And the rest, of course, is history.

To take another example, the founders of Purewater had been incubated within their engineering college and caught the interest of an angel investor during the incubator's pitch session. And from there to the angel network was a short journey.

Aman Garg of Greymeter fame followed a somewhat similar path, except that his company had gone through an accelerator and not an incubator. So Aman and his team were picked up in the accelerator's pitch session and invited to make a pitch at the angels' next meeting.

QACCO was a bit different. Chaitanya and Abhinav had a professor—me (Dhruv)—who happened to be an angel investor as well. They met me and I was impressed with their business model. And that's how they landed up at the next angel investors' meeting.

We could go on and on, but you get the point, don't you? There are several ways in which your start-up can connect with angel networks. However, irrespective of how this connect is made, there would be filtering involved—possibly multiple rounds of filtering—before you are actually allowed to make a pitch at an angel session.

What about VCs and Strategic Investors?

So far, we've spoken about angels and angel networks. But for VCs, the approach needs to be different. Yes, you could locate VCs on the Internet and send them your pitch deck, but the hit rate here is likely to be low. For one thing, VCs get tonnes of such requests and the likelihood of you getting shortlisted is not too high. Further, different VCs have different investment philosophies and until you fit into their philosophy, well, you'll simply end up in their recycle bin. Unfortunately.

Perhaps the best way to contact VCs is to give a mandate to an investment advisory service. These are firms that help you get investments at later stages—typically at the Series A stage and beyond. For their services they take a small percentage of the funds raised. And, in return, they use their contacts, do the first-level selling for you and hopefully get you a deal—including all the legalities that go along with it. They will also bring in super angels, and even strategic investors (those who view the investment as an extension to their existing business, rather than a purely financial one) wherever it makes sense. The biggest advantage with this approach, of course, is that it leaves you relatively free to run your business rather than be a full-time fundraiser!

The process followed by VCs is fairly similar to what you follow with angel networks—with two differences. First of all, meetings with VCs are one-on-one, rather than a presentation to a roomful of angels. And secondly, the business analysis as well as the due diligence tends to be far more rigorous. After all, the VC is putting in much more money—and that, too, at a higher valuation.

Either way, whether it's early stage to angels or later stage to VCs or strategic investors, the key is your pitch. But what exactly is a pitch? Very simply, it's your business plan which you 'pitch' to investors. What's your business, what's the market size, what's your entry barrier, how do you plan to scale up, etc. Sounds familiar? You're right, this is exactly the PERSISTENT framework that we have been shouting about right through this book. That's what investors want to see. Of course, they also want to see how much funding you need and what you plan to do with it. That, in a nutshell, is the business plan that you will be pitching to your potential investors.

What does this plan look like? Well, for that you'll have to wait a bit. Shut this book, go take a walk and perhaps have a few cups of coffee. We'll meet again in the next chapter.

17

Your PERSISTENT Business Plan

So we have finally reached the extremely important subject of your business plan. And how you need to pitch it to investors. Unfortunately many founders have only a vague idea of what a business plan is, and an even more vague idea of why they need it. So ladies and gentlemen, please fasten your seat belts. We are now going to learn all about business plans, what they contain, who needs them and why . . .

In very simple terms, a business plan is a document that describes the key aspects of your business: what you plan to do and how you plan to do it. Along with an Excel sheet that contains reasonably detailed financial projections for the next twelve–eighteen months and a broader picture of the next couple of years. It can also be outlined in the form of a PowerPoint presentation—perhaps with fifteen or twenty slides, along with the mandatory Excel sheet, of course. What do these slides cover? We're sure you know the answer by now. That's right, investors look for PERSISTENT start-ups to invest in. So your business plan must explain to them why your start-up fits into the PERSISTENT framework.

In addition, you would need to include a few other things. Your earnings model would have covered revenues and expenses so far, but you also need to give future projections for both. And then, of course, you must specify the amount of funding you need—something we call the 'ask'. Along with the valuation you are expecting. You must also specify what you will use this funding for. After all, the investor needs to know where his money will be going, doesn't he?

Now here's something very, very important. Is this business plan only meant for your investors? Of course not. Even more than investors, it's meant for you, Mr or Ms Founder. After all, you've got to have a plan before you start building your website. Or recruit people. Or splurge on marketing. In fact, before you do anything significant in your venture, you need to have a plan in place. So here goes . . .

All through this book we have introduced you to different founders and their start-ups. In this chapter we'll introduce you to another founder and his fascinating start-up. And, in the process, learn how to make a business plan. So please meet Rabindranath P. Rabindranath, a commerce graduate from Mumbai and a compulsive video-game enthusiast. Now his full name is rather cumbersome, so in this book we'll just use the far-more-compact Rabindranath Rabindranath. This young man had figured out a way to be involved with video games (which he loved) and earn money at the same time (which he also loved). The idea was simply this: If you are a gaming enthusiast, what happens to your old games once you get bored? Well, you simply push them deep into one of your cupboards and then buy new games. But that's expensive, isn't it? And, therefore, you cannot buy and play too many different games. It's just too costly. Now here's the key—what if Rabindranath Rabindranath were to buy off old video games from gamers? And then sell them at a higher price, to other gamers who had not yet played these games? Gamers would then be able to sell their old games to him and, with a bit of money added on, buy new games—those that someone else had traded in. Can you imagine the number of additional games they would now be able to play? Could any gaming enthusiast possibly ask for more? And, therefore, wasn't this a great business opportunity?

So Rabindranath Rabindranath decided to start a business venture, proudly called PlayMoreMore (as you can see, repeating a name was a family tradition). Where you could sell your old console games that you no longer wanted to play. And get credits in return, which you could then use to buy different games. A kind of 'games exchange'.

Once Rabindranath Rabindranath launched his venture, he came to us for funding. He explained his business to us and told us he needed funds to grow. But he wasn't sure how to create a business plan and approach investors. So we sat down with him and helped him create a business plan—largely over liberal cups of coffee at a local café in Mumbai. And what follows is the story of how this plan was created. Around the PERSISTENT framework, of course . . .

First things first. To create a successful business, you need to identify a PROBLEM for which you have a solution. In Rabindranath Rabindranath's case, the PROBLEM was clear: Gamers get bored of their old video games. And new ones were expensive. So they would love to sell their old games, pay a little extra and get new ones instead. Remember, to create a successful business, *you need to solve a real problem.* If you don't, you fall in the fascinating category of *solutions looking for problems.* And no, this is not a joke—we have seen several start-ups in this category.

To get back to Rabindranath Rabindranath, we then asked him about the SIZE OF THE MARKET. He was clear that the market for gamers was perhaps not huge but large enough—in other words, a reasonably large NICHE. And growing, as more and more young people got hooked to video games. Equally important, most gamers were addicted to gaming and unlikely to quit.

At this point, let's share with you what a typical early-stage investor looks for. Remember, the investor will get an exit only when he sells his stake to another investor in a future round of funding. And that second investor, in turn, looks at selling his stake to a third investor. And so on. Now this can only happen if investors at each stage see enough future growth, which rules out businesses that operate in a NICHE market. So did that mean curtains down for our young friend? Fortunately not. Because he could always start in a NICHE market, establish himself and then expand into the mainstream later on. For instance, he could move beyond games to laptops, phones and perhaps all electronic items over time. And so he was able to tick the SIZE OF THE MARKET box.

And now to the actual business he was running. We ordered another round of coffee and got down to his EARNINGS MODEL. You've seen this in most stories in this book, but since it is critically important, we'll show it to you one more time. Ultimately, every company must make a profit, whether it is a start-up or a giant such as Hindustan Unilever. In other words, the amount they earn must be higher than the amount they spend. But doesn't that leave you a bit confused? Just look around you, and you'll see lots of companies— including unicorns—growing rapidly but making a loss. Just open the pink papers and you'll see what we mean. And in spite of this, they keep getting funding—at higher and higher valuations. Looking at all this, what does our young founder think? 'Great—I'll also keep losing money, and grow rapidly. And I'll make it up through funding.' So he happily loses money. And you know what happens next, don't you? Most likely he doesn't get the funding he needs. And his start-up dies a swift, natural death!

Dear reader, please listen to us very carefully. There are easier and less painful ways to get your start-up to commit suicide. No business can survive without making money. Let's repeat that in big, bold letters—NO BUSINESS CAN SURVIVE WITHOUT MAKING MONEY. 'But what about all those unicorns around us?' you might say. 'They are not earning money, and they seem quite proud of it.' Quite right. They are not. But let's hold that question for a bit. Let's first understand this complex business of making money. You would have seen the term 'unit economics' in many of the stories in this book. But just to drive the point home, here it is again. Unit economics is essentially the money you make on each unit you sell. In Rabindranath Rabindranath's case, suppose he were buying old video games at an average of Rs 800 per game, which included the cost of picking up the game from the seller. And then selling them at an average price of Rs 1200, once again including the cost of delivering the game to the buyer. In this case, the unit economics of his business was positive, because he was making Rs 1200 minus Rs 800, or Rs 400 on each video game sold. In other words, the direct revenue from the sale of one unit minus the direct cost of that unit was positive. Please remember, the unit economics of your business must be positive, otherwise you will lose money on every unit you sell. And the more units you sell, the more you will lose!

Now here's the catch. Does the unit economics of your business have to be positive from Day 1? For instance, what if Rabindranath Rabindranath were to buy old video games at an average of Rs 800 as before, *but sell them at Rs 700?* Why would he do this? Maybe he wanted to get gamers hooked fast. And was therefore selling his games at a discount, with the intention of *increasing the price over time,* thereby making the unit economics positive. Makes sense, doesn't it? Several businesses start with negative unit economics to penetrate a new market or kick-start a new business. And that's perfectly acceptable to investors—provided, of course, that there is a plan to make it positive over time.

So much for unit economics. But assuming you've managed positive unit economics, is that enough to guarantee overall profitability in your business? Of course not. Remember, unit economics only covers the direct cost of selling a unit. It does not cover the overheads of the business—overheads such as rentals, marketing, salaries, etc. Let's continue with Rabindranath Rabindranath's example once again. As mentioned earlier, he was earning a margin of Rs 400 on every video game he sold. And let's further assume that he was selling an average of 100 video games a month. In other words, he was making a margin of Rs 100 x 400, or Rs 40,000 on these. Now if his rentals, marketing, salary costs and other overheads were, say, Rs 1 lakh a month, he would still be making a loss of

Rs 1 lakh minus Rs 40,000, or Rs 60,000 a month. In spite of great unit economics!

You see? Unit economics is just one of the conditions you need to satisfy to be profitable at the level of the company. You must also sell a sufficient number of units so that the total margin earned is higher than the total overheads. In this case, Rabindranath Rabindranath would need to sell 250 videos a month to get a total margin of Rs 250 x 400, or Rs 1 lakh, to cover his overheads, and therefore break even. He would become profitable only if the volumes were higher than this!

Now let's look at the investor's viewpoint. Believe it or not, investors are sane, reasonable people. First of all, they realize that your unit economics may not be positive early on in the business, when you are trying to penetrate the market. As long as they see this becoming positive over time, they are okay. While they would certainly like profitability at the company level, they are more concerned about growth and are willing to wait for profits. After all, the reason why anyone invests in a start-up is to see it reaching a dominant position in the market. Which can only happen if the company makes significant investments—whether in product development or sales or marketing. And these are overheads that will eat into profitability. *But this is acceptable to investors, provided—and this is a major provided— the start-up is growing at a rapid pace.* In a sense, investors are okay compromising on profitability to achieve growth.

Typically, when investors look at a business, they expect the unit economics to become positive over a short period of time, say one or two years. But they do not expect profitability at the company level so early. Three to four years or even longer in some cases is acceptable, provided, of course, there is rapid growth. These are very broad thumb rules—profitability could actually take much, much longer, particularly in a highly competitive space. And that, ladies and gentlemen, explains why all those biggies around us are still not making a profit and yet attracting investors. Meanwhile, the mad, mad growth story goes on . . .

Let's now get back to our friend Rabindranath Rabindranath. By now we've established the fact that his business satisfied our first few criteria—it was solving a real PROBLEM, the MARKET SIZE was not huge but a large enough NICHE, and the EARNINGS MODEL was positive—at least at the unit economics level. And then we got down to the next critical issue, namely SCALABILITY. Remember, MARKET SIZE is meaningless unless you can SCALE up rapidly within this market. After all, why else would investors be interested in your venture?

Now SCALING is a highly misunderstood term among start-ups. Let's take an example. Suppose you were to start a swanky new barber's shop in some locality. So you take a place on rent, do up the interiors and recruit the appropriate staff—in other words, you invest both time and capital in setting up shop. Question: Is this a SCALABLE business? Of course not. Even if it does well, it can at best reach a revenue of a few lakh rupees per annum. And then it stagnates, because there isn't enough capacity. Now if you were to add capacity by starting one more such unit, you would need to take another place on rent, do it up once again and recruit more staff. More capital and more time. And your revenues simply go up by a few more lakhs per annum. And so on . . .

How do we make this business SCALABLE? Suppose instead that you were to build a website and get barbers across the city to enlist on it. Further let's assume that each barber specializes in a different kind of hairstyle—from Johnny Depp to Brad Pitt to a Mohawk. Now if a customer is bored with his current hairstyle and wants a different look, what would he do? Well, he would probably go to this website, search for the appropriate barber and finally book an appointment through you. For which you would get a commission. And that, my friend, is a SCALABLE business.

What's the key difference between these two business models? In the first one, for every few lakhs of revenue that you wanted to earn, you would need to add manpower, space and therefore money. And, of course, it would take time. But in the second model, once you had the website up and running and a call centre for support, you would not need to keep adding any of these for every few lakhs of revenue. Other than the addition of server capacity, once your volumes became too large to handle. And that's the difference between a SCALABLE and a NON-SCALABLE business. In a NON-SCALABLE business, you need to keep adding resources every time you want to increase your revenues by a small amount. But in a SCALABLE business, once you've invested in it, there are no significant incremental resources required.

How does this apply to our friend Rabindranath Rabindranath? Very simple—his business of buying and selling video games was not manpower-dependent and he didn't need additional offices to grow either. Verdict? SCALABLE.

And then, of course, there are the RISKS of running the business. Now here we must make an important observation. Many founders simply gloss over their risks. Either they're highly optimistic and have therefore not thought about them, or perhaps they do not want to disclose these RISKS to potential investors. After all, they wouldn't want to scare them away, would they? But that's a terrible policy. Just to drive the point home, let's repeat it—*it is a terrible, terrible policy.* Investors are aware that every business has its share of RISKS. For instance, a key RISK faced by any start-up is the RISK of a large player with deep pockets squeezing it out through hefty discounts. Fintech companies would run the RISK of changing RBI policies, which might make their entire business model unviable. And so on. Now if you stand in front of investors claiming that there aren't any RISKS in your business, they would get the message that you haven't analysed your business in any great detail. Or worse, are trying to fool them—and that's guaranteed to put them off! Investors accept the fact that each business will have RISKS. They simply want to make sure that you have understood them and have a strategy in place to mitigate them. So be honest—clearly mention the RISKS involved, along with your strategy to tackle them.

What was the key RISK in Rabindranath Rabindranath's start-up? Simply this: the possibility of much large players in the area of buying and selling used products (such as Cashify and OLX) getting interested in the NICHE area of games. And therefore squeezing him out, perhaps through discounting. Now if you've been reading this book carefully, you would have realized that he needed an ENTRY BARRIER, which would make it tougher for such players to displace him. Was discounting one such ENTRY BARRIER? Of course not. A bigger player with deeper pockets can always give bigger discounts. *But one thing the bigger player cannot do is to quickly acquire a large number of customers in a space they have not been in so far.* They would need to market themselves in this space, and gamers would take time to shift loyalties. So now you begin to see Rabindranath Rabindranath's strategy. What he was trying to do was SCALE up rapidly and acquire a large customer base of gamers. And that would be his ENTRY BARRIER.

By the way, there is another interesting possible twist to this story. Suppose one of these larger players did want to enter this market. Rather than starting from scratch and building up their presence over time, they could simply buy out PlayMoreMore, couldn't they? Or make a large investment in the company. So rather than competing with this larger player, PlayMoreMore would actually get absorbed into them. Funding would not be a problem now and Rabindranath Rabindranath's early investors would get a fat exit. In other words, everyone would be happy.

While on the subject of ENTRY BARRIERS, there is one more thing that we must talk about—and that is INNOVATION. Any INNOVATION in your product or business model usually results in a high ENTRY BARRIER, and therefore gets potential investors really excited. Of course, if you have a patent or two, that's really great! You saw how Uno Finance used analytics to de-risk their loans to potential patients. Or how Samant Sikka SQRRLed away little bits of money from your daily or weekly spend to make saving painless. So if you have INNOVATIVE solutions, please ensure that they are put across to investors loud and clear.

Often INNOVATION comes from the use of technology—
which was the case in both the above examples. Now here we must
share with you an interesting experience we had with one young
founder, who wanted our advice:

'Sir, how do I bring "blockchain technology" into my start-up?'

You can imagine our reaction. 'Why do you need to bring it in?'

'Well, I've heard that investors are keen to invest in emerging
technologies such as blockchain. It will definitely increase our
chances of getting funding. And raise our valuation as well,' was the
somewhat innocent answer.

You get the message, don't you? Incidentally, this is not an
isolated incident. Several founders try and bring in INNOVATIVE
technology *just for the sake of bringing it in,* and not because it has any
meaningful impact on the business. In the recent past, we have come
across many founders who have very proudly shown us how they have
used the latest buzzwords such as blockchain, machine learning and
augmented reality in their business. But were these really required?
Unfortunately, no. These technologies were brought in simply to
make the business look more INNOVATIVE and sexy. Obviously,
investors will see through such gimmicks. So use INNOVATIVE
technology, by all means, but not as a gimmick. Use it to add real
value to your business.

The other important issue that investors evaluate is the TEAM,
starting with the founders. In fact, it is often said that early-stage
investors invest predominantly in the founders rather than in the
business, since it is usually too early to evaluate the business anyway.
And good founders will be able to pivot or modify the business model
if required. What do investors look for in the founding TEAM?
Well, their vision for the project, their qualifications, their level of
experience, knowledge about the area, confidence, clarity of thought,
etc. And, above all, their passion. Because if there is one thing that
carries you through hard times—and there *will* be hard times—it
is passion. Of course, Rabindranath Rabindranath qualified on
most counts.

And now for the meaty part—the numbers. The investors would certainly like to see the TRACTION you have achieved. But they are even more interested in the future, and the past is simply an indication of what the future might be. Importantly, they are likely to ask you for two sets of figures—what you will achieve if you get the funding, and what if you don't. And what's your 'go-to market' strategy to achieve these numbers. As an example, in the QACCO story, our founders had decided to use the B2B2C strategy, and therefore planned to target HR executives in large organizations to get their employees onboarded. A very neat, low-cost 'go-to market' strategy. Or take a look at SQRRL—apart from digital marketing, Samant was making presentations across colleges to catch the college crowd. Rabindranath Rabindranath, of course, wanted gamers, and therefore he decided on digital marketing on gaming sites. Along with word of mouth—after all, gamers were known to be a close-knit community and people who were happy would refer their friends to PlayMoreMore. To summarize, therefore, you must project your month-by-month numbers, including revenues, and how you plan to achieve them.

What else? Remember, we have been talking about the EARNINGS MODEL right through—and that includes both revenues and costs. So you need to talk about costs—salaries, rentals, marketing costs, operational costs, etc. In other words, you would need to create an Excel sheet that contains month-wise revenues as well as costs.

Let's take a look at what Rabindranath Rabindranath's projections would look like:

	Mth 1	Mth 2	Mth 3	Mth 4	Mth 5	Mth 6	Mth 7	Mth 8	Mth 9
Number of Active Customers									
Number of Games Sold									
Total Revenues									
Number of Games Bought									
Cost of Games Bought									
Cost—Salaries									
Cost—Marketing									
Cost—Operations									
Total Costs									
Burn (Total Costs – Total Revenues)									
Cumulative Burn									

We must also tell you that investors do not see these projections as iron-clad and written in blood. They are smart and have dealt with several start-ups in the past. They realize that the future is uncertain and that assumptions can go wrong, especially with disruptive start-ups. What they really want to see is not the mathematical accuracy of your projections but your understanding of the business and the market you operate in. And, of course, your ability to change course or pivot whenever required. Figures are taken with a pinch—or perhaps a tablespoon—of salt.

By the way, it is important to remember that funding can never be guaranteed. And what happens if you don't get it? Do you simply close down your terrific start-up and walk into the nearest bar to drown your sorrows? No, my friend, you need to get into survival mode. Cut costs where you can, do not invest for huge growth, and try and become profitable at the level of the company. Even if your growth slows to a trickle. Because you are now in survival and not growth mode. Which really means that you need to have a back-up business plan for survival—where you are at least making enough money to sustain your business, till funding ultimately comes through. Remember, *funding is generally given for growth, and not for survival.*

Of course, there are exceptions to this rule. If you are in the SQRRL kind of business, where you are not really looking at revenues initially, you would need repeated funding. Or if your business is based on the development of a product or a prototype that requires a lot of capital before your revenues start flowing in. But, in general, remember that investors like companies that can survive on their own, but need their funds for growth.

Okay, so we've discussed lots and lots of the stuff that goes into a business plan. But that's not all. You need to specify how much money you need and at what valuation. And, of course, what you will do with the money. Oh—we almost forgot—we also need to discuss the powerful concept of WYKM. And . . .

But that's a lot of things to discuss. We thought you'd be tired by now. So we decided to give you a break. And look at them in a fresh, new chapter—the next one.

Bye till then . . .

18

Your Business Plan—the Finishing Touches

Welcome back from your well-deserved break. So far we have seen how you can create a business plan around our favourite PERSISTENT framework. And now let's give the finishing touches to this plan, with some extremely important pieces, starting with the concept of 'ask'.

What's Your Ask? And What's Your Runway?

That's one of the most obvious questions any investor would have—how much money do you need? In other words, what's your 'ask'? Plus, of course, what you will do with this money. After all, no investor is going to give you lakhs—or perhaps crores—and say, 'We like your face, so here's the money you wanted. Do what you want with it.' That's not the way it works, my friend. Investors need to understand how you will spend their hard-earned money before they part with it. How much you would put into product development, how much into sales and marketing, how much into operations, or any other major expense heads. And only once they are convinced will they reach for their chequebooks.

So how do you figure out your 'ask'? Actually, it's fairly simple. Just go back to the table in the previous chapter, where you had made your projections, and take a look at the last two rows. The second-last row, or 'burn', is the gap between what you are spending and what you are earning each month. If you want to survive—and we certainly hope you do—this gap needs to be bridged through funding. Now let's understand another term, namely 'runway'. Obviously you are familiar with a runway at an airport. The crucial issue here is that an aeroplane can only taxi as far as the runway. Before the runway ends, it needs to take off. So what's the parallel with your projections? Simply this—your funding gives you a runway, and before you come to the end of that runway you need to get more money. Which either means that you need to become profitable or you need more funding.

How do you figure out your runway? Well, for this you need two figures. First of all, the amount of funding you're raising—and let's assume it's a crore. Secondly, the last row of the projections in the table in the previous chapter—namely the 'cumulative burn'. Now assume that your cumulative burn reaches a crore by Month 10, after which it crosses a crore. By now we're sure you've figured out the runway—it's ten months. In other words, the month by which your cumulative burn reaches the amount of funds you're raising is your runway. After that there is no money to take care of the burn. Conversely, if you want your runway to be at least one year, you need to look at the cumulative burn at the end of a year. And that, ladies and gentlemen, is your 'ask'. That's the funding you need! By the way, we strongly recommend that your runway be at least a year and a half, so that you don't end up chasing money all the time instead of managing your business. And since this is important, we've put it down as a formula:

'Ask' = 'Cumulative burn' at the end of the 'runway'

While on the subject of business projections, here's a practical tip. Investors need an exit, and that, too, at a higher valuation—after all, that's why they invested in your company in the first place, didn't they? And for this, you will need to grow rapidly so as to interest the next-level investor. Therefore, you show high revenues in your Excel sheet. Obviously, for this you will need to spend— on the product, on operations, on marketing, etc. And that means a high 'ask'. But at this early stage, you are not likely to get this kind of 'ask'. So you moderate your sales projections and look for a lower 'ask'. However, you will now definitely not get any funding, because investors are not interested in a moderately growing company. So you increase the 'ask'. But then again, it might be too high. And so on . . .

As you can see, making your business projections is an iterative process. And ultimately, you need to strike a balance between the sales projections and the 'ask'. Of course, if you can reduce the 'ask' by running a frugal operation, that's even better!

At this point, you also need to understand the concept of multi-tranche investments. Let's go back to MyCuteOffice for a moment. Suppose Abhishek had said that he wanted funding to expand within Mumbai, and subsequently to Delhi, Bengaluru, Chennai and Hyderabad, and for all this he needed Rs 4 crore. What do you think the investors would have said? Most likely they would have looked at each other with a knowing smile and said, 'Look, we can't take that kind of risk at this stage. You take what you need for Mumbai right now. Prove that you can scale up, and then we'll give you more for the other cities. In other words, we'll give you the money in two tranches. Based on the first tranche, let's set a milestone. Once you meet that, we'll release the second tranche. By the way, the second tranche could even be at a higher valuation.' Incidentally, this is not an informal arrangement. It actually becomes part of the term sheet and ultimately the shareholder agreement.

Before we end the subject of 'ask', let's share a couple of thumb rules with you. When your business is just a few months old and clear traction is not visible, what do you think you are likely to get?

Well, around a crore is a reasonable figure to work with, which you can use to prove your business model. Of course, if you can't and your start-up bombs, you may need to quietly register with Naukri.com and scour its portal, frantically looking for opportunities. But let's be optimistic—we know it'll work out. And with this funding, you would probably have established some trends, with a clear month-on-month or quarter-on-quarter growth. Also, you would have achieved some level of market penetration. At this stage, you can definitely look at raising more—typically Rs 2–3 crore—for further growth. Once even that is achieved, the purse strings really begin to loosen up, so you can raise a round of perhaps Rs 7–10 crore. Or if you prefer, a million dollars (sounds so much more impressive, doesn't it—even if every penny of this amount comes in rupees). And so on . . .

The Simple Subject of Valuation

Aha! Valuation is one of the most fuzzy issues in raising funds. But the concept itself is fairly simple. It's the total value of a company. In other words, if a company has a valuation of Rs 3 crore and you planned to buy all the shares in the company, you would have to shell out Rs 3 crore. That's it.

Now suppose this company were to raise Rs 1 crore from investors. Before the fund raise, the valuation of the company was Rs 3 crore. After the fund raise, the company has an additional 1 crore of cash. Therefore, the valuation goes up to Rs 3+1 crore = Rs 4 crore. And the terms we use for this are 'pre-money' valuation and 'post-money' valuation. Obvious, isn't it? In general, therefore, whenever a company raises funds, the following equation holds true:

'Post Money Valuation' = 'Pre-Money Valuation' + 'Ask'

Next question: Who owns how much of the company? Well, in this example, before the fund raise, the founders owned 100 per cent of the company, or Rs 3 crore. After the fund raise, they still own Rs 3 crore worth of shares, *but in a company which is now valued at Rs 4 crore*. So they now own 75 per cent of the company. And by the same logic, the investors own Rs 1 crore out of Rs 4 crore, or 25 per cent of the company. How will this be implemented? Well, the founders will issue new shares to the investors in the same proportion.

Dear founder, we realize that we are getting into complex mathematics, but you'll have to be patient for a bit more. Assume the company had issued 10,000 shares of Rs 10 each to the founders, prior to the funding. After the fund raise, these original 10,000 shares will now comprise 75 per cent of the total shares in the company. In other words, after the fund raise, the revised number of shares in the company will be 10,000 ÷ 75 per cent, or 13,333 shares. And, therefore, we have another simple formula:

'Total number of shares after the fund raise' – 'Original number of shares' = 'Number of shares to be issued to the investors'
In our case, this works out to 13,333 - 10,000 = 3,333

The founders now hold 10,000 out of 13,333 shares, or 75 per cent of the company. And the investors hold 3,333 out of 13,333 shares, or 25 per cent. What's the price at which the investors get their shares? As you can see, they have paid Rs 1 crore, or Rs 1,00,00,000, for 3,333 shares. So the price at which they have got each share is Rs 1,00,00,000 ÷ 3,333, which works out to Rs 3,000.3 per share. And, by the way, that's the end of our session on complex mathematics!

So we've seen that the concept of valuation is reasonably straightforward. But what is definitely not straightforward is how to figure out the valuation at which funds are raised. In fact, we'll go a step further—this is perhaps the most complex and least understood subject in the whole area of fundraising.

Why?

Read on . . .

The Unbelievably Complex Subject of Determining Valuation

Seasoned investors, who disagree violently on most issues, are unanimous on one point: namely that there is no formula for valuation. Yes, there are thumb rules and there are tips, but definitely no formula. And ultimately, the valuation of a start-up is what the investors and founders negotiate over a cup of coffee—or perhaps a somewhat stiffer drink to soften up the founder. Hardened investors do not get softened up, you see.

But hang on. We are getting ahead of ourselves, so let's first get deeper into the fascinating subject of valuation. In conventional companies, valuation is usually arrived at by estimating the company's future profits in each subsequent year and then applying a standard formula. Obviously, higher profits would mean higher valuations.* Now what we are about to say is important, so please listen carefully: To estimate future profits, you first need to look at the past. You can then make assumptions to figure out how these past profits can be projected into the future. Unfortunately, even for large, stable companies, past profits are usually ambiguous. For instance, if a company has launched a major advertising campaign, do they count these expenses within one year or do they amortize them over three years? For revenue calculations, do they use invoicing or accrued revenue? And so on. Therefore past profits are, and will remain, somewhat ambiguous, depending on the accounting policies adopted by the organization. And now for the future. If the company had been growing its profit figures by, say, 15 per cent every year, it is perhaps reasonable to assume that this will continue. But what if the past performance of the company had been erratic? How do we project their earnings? Or what if the market is depressed in

---

* For financial wizards, this method is known as the DCF, or the discounted cash flow technique. For mere mortals, just remember that it is broadly based on future profit projections.

the future? Would our company still be able to grow at 15 per cent per year? So on top of the ambiguous past profits, there are several question marks when projecting them into the future. Which means the valuation can at best be a range. However, given the fact that the company had a past, there is still some basis for figuring out the valuation.

Now let's get down to our favourite companies—start-ups. No past. And just to push the point home, we'll repeat it: *They have no past.* Even if they do have a bit of a past, they would perhaps have pivoted their business model a couple of times, so we really cannot project the past into the future. You see, the world of start-ups is tumultuous, with uncertainty being the only certainty. On top of that, there is almost no past. And even if there is, there are no profits, in most cases. So how do you project future profits? And how do you figure out the valuation of the company?

The answer, my friend—as Bob Dylan said in his famous song—is blowing in the wind. You simply cannot. There is no formula to determine valuations in start-ups. Fortunately, however, there are thumb rules, which work at least some of the time— and that's about the best we can get. One obvious thumb rule is to compare the company with others in the same industry. For instance, small SaaS (software as a service) companies are typically valued at five–six times their annual revenues. But what if there is no revenue? Or at best pilots? And anyway, such data is not easy to access—remember, these companies are not listed on any stock exchange.

The other guideline for companies that have already raised some funding earlier is to look at the valuation in the earlier round. And then adjust this valuation for what happened subsequently. For instance, high growth over the last round would push up the valuation and, by the same logic, de-growth would pull it down.

Another method used is to work backwards from the 'ask' and figure out how much stake the founder is willing to give up. And, by the same logic, what stake the investors would get in the company. So if the ask is Rs 1 crore and the founder agrees to part with 10 per cent of the company, this automatically leads to a post-money valuation of Rs 10 crore and a pre-money valuation of Rs 9 crore. Incidentally, this is one of the most common guidelines used. Also, a stake dilution of 10–15 per cent is fairly common in the first round of funding.

By the way, some experienced angels have worked out an interesting thumb rule to determine valuations, which we've shown in the form of the following table:

Status of the Start-Up	Pre-Money Valuation
Concept level with perhaps a successful pilot	Rs 4–6 crore
Some history of revenues	Rs 8–10 crore
Significant history of revenues	Rs 12–15 crore

Of course, these are ballpark figures and can vary depending on the situation.

As you might have guessed, there are several factors that impact the valuation of a start-up, both positively and negatively. And most of these are linked to—you've guessed it—our good old PERSISTENT framework. For instance, if you have a significant ENTRY BARRIER, you get a higher valuation. If you've been able to achieve significant TRACTION, you again get a higher valuation. Or if you are a James Bond among founders, you again get a higher valuation. But, ultimately, please remember that this is a demand-and-supply issue. If you are chasing many investors and are desperate, your valuation goes down. On the other hand, if your start-up is highly in demand and investors are chasing you instead, your valuation goes a bit higher—and we sincerely hope this is the case.

Finally, let's end this section with something really poetic: 'Beauty and valuation both lie in the eyes of the beholder.'

Don't Get Stuck on Valuations

Having given you all this hefty 'gyan' about 'ask' and valuations—
and perhaps got you royally confused—let's take a few stories to
figure out what you should do. As usual, remember that these are
guidelines and not rules, so please use your common sense in making
a decision. And don't blame us if things go wrong.

Our first story deals with Andatoast.com—a fictitious name, as
you might imagine. Started by a young founder, P.K. Breakfastwala,
known as PK to his friends, the company used to deliver items
typically used at breakfast time, such as bread, eggs, milk, sausages,
etc. And of course, the orders were placed online. PK's focus was
small towns, and he needed Rs 50 lakh to expand his network. He
fondly believed that his company deserved a pre-money valuation
of Rs 10 crore. Sadly, the investors believed otherwise and he
finally got his funding at a pre-money valuation of Rs 4.5 crore,
or Rs 450 lakh. In other words, he had parted with 50 / (450+50)
or 10 per cent of his company. As you can imagine, PK didn't
know whether to be happy or sad. But hang on—just listen to the
rest of the story. These funds came in at just the right time for
him, because he was able to invest in marketing, in operations,
and in his platform to make it more user-friendly. And guess what?
Andatoast.com grew rapidly and began to attract eyeballs from the
investor community. PK was able to raise a full crore in the next
round, at a pre-money valuation of Rs 19 crore, or a post-money
valuation of a high Rs 20 crore. And in the process, he was on a
terrific growth path.

Before we analyse this story, let's also look at PK's competitor—
Nashta.com, started by CK, but in a different small town. CK faced
a similar situation, but he wasn't willing to raise money at a low
valuation. So he decided to cut costs and bootstrap. And what do you
think happened? Given the cost constraints, Nashta.com grew very
slowly. And over time, investors lost interest in it. So it is still alive,
but no one really cares . . .

And now for a third story—that of Blockchaindada.com. We don't really need to share details of the business these guys were in, but the point is that they were able to raise a crore of funds at a hefty post-money valuation of Rs 12 crore. Clearly the founders were overjoyed and celebrated repeatedly in a nearby pub. Unfortunately, however, the business did not grow as expected, because the market was slow to catch on to their idea. Anyhow, that is not the point. The point is that that these guys did raise a next round of Rs 2 crore, but *at a lower valuation of Rs 10 crore,* post-money. Something that we call a *down round.* So while the founders were celebrating their bonanza after the first round, they actually had to shell out a larger chunk of the company in the second round.

In this case, there is another interesting issue. Most savvy investors—and we haven't really met dumb ones—would insert a cute 'anti-dilution clause' in the shareholder agreement. Which means that if the company raises funds at a lower valuation in future, these original investors would get additional shares free of cost, in such a way that the average valuation of their total shares is equal to the new valuation. So the original investors are protected. In other words, even though the founders of Blockchaindada celebrated after the first round of funding, after the second round, the original valuation was brought down. Interesting, isn't it?

What's the message from these three stories? Well, first of all, *if you need funding to grow rapidly, you need it.* Do not worry too much about the valuation and the stake you are letting go. Obviously you must try and get the best deal you can, *but get the funding.* It'll help you grow rapidly, and your next round can then be at a significantly higher valuation. So while you may have parted with a significant stake in the first round, you can actually get far more for a proportionately lower stake in the next round. Conversely, you may have got a very high valuation in the first round, but in the next one, it could actually come down, and anyway you will most likely have to issue fresh shares to the original investors. Remember, over time valuations tend to align more and more with the business, and have less to do with the negotiating ability of both sides. And, therefore, raise the money if you need to, without worrying too much about the valuation!

The Impact of the Coronavirus—or Any Other Crisis

Dear reader, perhaps the first thing that is impacted by any crisis is valuation. Obvious, isn't it? Whether it is the COVID-19 crisis, or the dot-com bust of the early 2000s, or even the global financial crisis of 2008, money becomes scarce. Investors turn risk-averse. And you'll have to really coax and cajole them into putting their hard-earned money into your venture. Even if they are willing, the chances are that they will insist on a lower valuation—so as to protect their downside risk. Now, of course, it is your call. Perhaps you can manage without raising funds at this stage by cutting costs and getting into survival mode. But then you might be losing an opportunity, isn't it? Alternatively, you could raise a smaller amount than originally planned, but at a lower valuation, which is acceptable to the investors.

There is another interesting option. Raise the money right now, without fixing the valuation at the moment. Instead, link it to the subsequent round of funding. How does this work? Well, let's call this Funding Round 1. And at some stage you will be raising Funding Round 2. You could then set the valuation in Round 1 at a 20 per cent discount (or any percentage that both sides can agree to) to the valuation arrived at in Round 2. In case you think you'll get a decent valuation in Round 2, this is an interesting option and is used quite often. By the way, this approach is also used when there is no crisis, in situations where the investors and the founders are not able to agree on the valuation.

And that brings us to the end of the business plan.

But now for the real thing. How do you pitch it to investors?

Aren't you excited? So are we. And we're just itching to have you turn the page . . .

19

Pitching Your Business Plan

The Concept of WYKM

So you've figured out your business plan, and decided on the 'ask' and the valuation. And you're all set to make your pitch. Not so fast, my friend. There is still one essential thing you need to take care of. Let's start with a question: How often have you seen packed PowerPoint presentations? Really packed ones? Lots and lots of slides, each packed with lots of text and perhaps some figures. And what do you get from such a presentation? Nothing? Too much data? Are you confused? What's the presenter trying to say? Or do you simply let your mind switch off—after all, the presentation has to end sometime . . .

Unfortunately, this is what most presentations look like. Too many ideas, too much text, and far, far too much for the audience to absorb. What's the natural consequence? The audience does not absorb anything. Or worse, they may absorb something trivial, which is not what you were trying to highlight anyway. What a terrible waste of an opportunity!

By the way, this is true of any communication exercise and not just presentations. You may be sitting across the table with a client and you bombard him with lots and lots of details. And what does he retain from all this? Perhaps nothing. Or, in the worst case, something trivial again. And he misses the main issue that you were trying to put across.

Remember, *communication is not just what the communicator wants to say. Communication is what the recipient receives, and ultimately absorbs and remembers.* Makes sense? So let's take a few examples:

- Maggi two-minute noodles
- *Achhe din aane wale hain* (Prime Minister Narendra Modi in his 2014 campaign)
- Yes, we can (Barack Obama)
- The Fevicol ad series, which communicates the fact that Fevicol makes things stick

We can take lots of other examples, but, for the moment, let's just focus on these four. You would definitely agree that these are very powerful messages. But what is common to these four?

Think, think . . .

That's right, each of these messages communicates one simple idea. Take a minute and read these messages again. You see what we mean? One simple, key idea. Which is easy to understand, absorb and, therefore, remember. Nothing huge, not hundreds of words, or tens of ideas. One simple message—that's it. And therefore, ladies and gentlemen, the recipient gets the message and remembers it!

We have a term for this very important concept in communication. We call it WYKM, which is short for 'WHAT'S YOUR KEY MESSAGE?'. This concept is critical to any good communication, and therefore to your presentation as well. Let's try and apply it to the start-ups we have met in this book so far. What would the WYKM for MyCuteOffice be? Perhaps 'Affordable co-working spaces'. What about QACCO? Maybe a slightly longer WYKM as follows, 'We make it easy to locate affordable holiday packages in boutique hotels.' Or let's take SQRRL. Something like, 'We make it easy to save money in micro-instalments. And we also help you invest it.' And, finally, what about Rabindranath Rabindranath's WYKM? Possibly, 'Exchange your old video game for a new one', or 'You'll always have a new video game'. Or even the short and simple, 'Play more, pay less.'

Get the idea? Each of these WYKMs has a very simple, hard-hitting and easy-to-remember message. Sometimes two simple messages. Now how do you apply this concept? Well, you as the founder need to decide what your WYKM is. And ensure that this gets communicated in your presentation. Preferably multiple times so the message hits home and the recipient remembers it. That's it. If there is one thing anyone remembers from your presentation, it should be your WYKM!

Now that you are armed with the requisite tools, you are all set to make your pitch, in the form of a presentation, as follows. We'll leave out details, since we've discussed those enough times. Please remember, this is only a guideline. No one will kill you if, say, you were to split Slide 3 into two slides or combine slides 4 and 5 into one. Also, remember, you should not have too much text in your presentation. No one reads pages and pages of text. Instead, have more figures and graphics wherever you can—that makes it far easier to follow the presentation. So here it is:

Slide 1: Title slide
Slide 2: The problem and the opportunity
Slide 3: Size of the market
Slide 4: The solution and scalability
Slide 5: Your earnings model
Slide 6: Innovation and entry barriers
Slide 7: Competition
Slide 8: Team (starting with the founders)
Slide 9: Traction so far
Slide 10: Projections
Slide 11: Ask and valuation

Got it? Great—so please start building your business plan—and all the best when you pitch it to investors!

Pitching to Angels—What Next?

Okay, you've now made your pitch to the angels. What happens after this? Actually, there are several steps—and we'll share with you what happens in a typical angel network. There may be variations, but this is generally the process followed. During the pitch, the angels figure out whether or not your start-up is of interest. If it is, well done. You've just crossed a major hurdle. They will then appoint one or two 'deal leads' to take the transaction further. These are investors who will evaluate your business in detail and then make their recommendations to the others. After all, you don't expect them to put in money based on a fifteen-minute presentation, do you? So the deal leads will study your business, meet customers, take feedback from the market, scour all the financials you have presented, etc. Of course, they will also negotiate the valuation, and perhaps suggest a two-tranche investment. And when they are satisfied, they will report back to the rest of the angels in the network. Subsequently, they are likely to arrange a conference call, where interested investors call in. Along with the deal leads and, of course, you guys as the founders. One more round of grilling follows (not easy to get money, is it?). And once you are nicely grilled and roasted, the network asks the angels to make their commitments in writing. And, by the way, congrats—you've crossed yet another hurdle. You will now sign a term sheet with the angel network. Essentially, this lays down the terms of the investment (more about this in the next chapter). And then starts the detailed process of 'due diligence', or simply DD. Where the network will get their accountants, company secretaries and lawyers to examine your company in detail. Have you filed all statutory details? Are your accounts in order? Are there any pending liabilities that the investors need to know about? Are there any pending issues with the government? Remember, the deal leads examined the business, but these guys will check whether you are following the law of the land while running it.

Once the DD is over, assuming you still have the energy to go ahead, there is the 'small' issue of the shareholder agreement to be made out. Which is a detailed version of the term sheet (see next chapter). Enter the lawyers once again. And when even this is over, all the shareholders as well as founders sign it and the money that was earlier committed flows in. Obviously, if the DD doesn't work out, the deal falls through—but we hope that doesn't happen to you.

Just to summarize, here are the steps that take place from the time you make your pitch to the time you get the funds:

1. Make your pitch to investors.
2. If your start-up is of interest, the investors appoint one or two deal leads who study your business in detail.
3. If satisfied, the founder and investors sign a term sheet, and commitments for investment are taken.
4. The investors now do legal as well as financial due diligence.
5. The shareholder agreement is signed.
6. Finally, you get your money.

Pitching to VCs

All along, we have been talking about pitching to a group of investors—typically angels. But what about subsequent investments, where you are pitching to VCs? Would that be significantly different?

Actually yes—the focus of the business plan will be a little different. In the angel round, you need to show potential with some proof. Proof that you satisfy the PERSISTENT framework that successful companies follow. Things like size of the market, scalability, execution capability of the team and all the other factors that go with being PERSISTENT. Of course, you would need to show some traction as well.

But in the Series A round and beyond, when you are facing VCs, potential is simply not enough. No sir, you've got your angel funding, and you've had time to build your business. Now you will clearly need to discuss numbers. You must show growth month on month, or at least quarter on quarter. And the unit economics needs to be positive. The VC must also be convinced that your venture can scale rapidly—which also means that the market size needs to be very large. Remember, when you approach angels, you do not have much of a past and, therefore, a lot of decisions are based on gut feeling. But with VCs, you need hard data.

The Impact of the Coronavirus—or Any Other Crisis

For a moment, put yourself in the shoes of a potential investor after such a crisis. If he is a businessman, his business is likely to have suffered. And his priority would be to resurrect it. If he is a stock market investor, he could easily have seen his wealth eroded significantly. In any case, he is probably extremely worried about the health and safety of his family . . .

We could go on and on. But you get the message, don't you? The investor has something else on his mind when he listens to your pitch. Now, is that a problem? My friend, it's really a huge opportunity if only you can use it. Try and link your pitch to the investor's thinking. So if your start-up has anything to do with health or home deliveries or online education, it fits in beautifully with his current worries. If there is a financial crisis of the kind that took place in 2008 and your start-up is into either saving money (such as SQRRL) or safe investing, make this the core of your pitch. If there has just been a major cyberattack and you are into online security solutions, once again you are in business.

By the way, this can also work with events that are positive in nature. For instance, during the Indian Premier League, the investor's mind is likely to be on cricket and anything to do with online gaming is likely to go down well with him.

So that was all about creating a business plan and pitching it to investors. We do hope you are able to raise the funding you need. And at the end of this gruelling exercise, all you want is to go on a nice relaxing vacation—perhaps take a cruise. But you can't, my friend, you've got a company to run, and now you've got shareholders to satisfy as well. So happy running, and all the best.

20

The 'Fun' World of Shareholder Agreements

Ladies and gentlemen, behold our 'fun' chapter. This is where we get into legal jargon and explain what goes into the shareholder agreement—the one you sign with your investors. Now a shareholder agreement is usually drafted by an army of lawyers that the investors have at their disposal—and obviously whetted by your lawyer as well. Most of it will sound like Greek to you—if not Swahili. But you must understand the key terms and clauses that go into it. And that is what we have tried to explain here. Please remember, however, that this chapter will not equip you to get an LLB degree. It is just to make you understand what you are putting your signature on. So here goes . . .

Shareholder Agreement and Term Sheet

It should be obvious what the 'shareholder agreement', or SHA, is. It's an agreement that the founders and investors sign when the investors put money in the company, and therefore become shareholders. Incidentally, the term investor can refer to anyone—angels, VCs or even strategic investors. Now, as we had mentioned in Chapter 16, the SHA is signed right at the end, when the due diligence is done and the money is about to flow in. But hang on—shouldn't we have had some sort of an MoU earlier? Once the deal leads have done the business analysis and the angels have taken a decision to invest? In fact, there is something like this, and it is called a 'term sheet'. Which is a simplified version of the shareholder agreement—enough to capture the key issues discussed, but minus the details. The way it works is that the investors issue a draft term sheet, based on which the two sides negotiate hard. Assuming they arrive at agreed terms, the term sheet is signed on behalf of the company by the founders and typically one representative of the angel network or the authorized signatory of the VC fund. By the way, we have included a sample term sheet in the appendix, just for your bedtime reading!

Director or Board Observer

The board of directors of a company is a powerful body, where all major decisions—other than operational ones—are taken. Look at it this way. All shareholders are owners of the company. Now if the managing director of this corporation wants to launch a new line of business, he must first check with the owners. But does that mean he needs to go down on bended knees and beg each shareholder to approve it? That's impossible, isn't it? After all, there may be lakhs of such shareholders. Even in a start-up, there could be twenty or even fifty shareholders. Fortunately, there is a simpler solution to the problem. Where all the shareholders elect a board of directors, which takes decisions on their behalf. Typically decisions on the direction the company is taking, its plans, as well as a review of these plans. And, of course, approving the balance sheet as well as the profit-and-loss account of the company. Only for a few decisions does the board need to take the approval of other shareholders—such as the issue of new shares, declaration of dividend and merger with another company.

These procedures are rigorously followed in large, well-managed organizations. However, start-ups do this far more informally. But there's one extremely important thing to remember if you are the founder of a company—and therefore on the board of directors. The directors of a company are responsible for paying statutory dues such as provident fund and taxes. If you don't, well, you will be fined, and could even end up in a nice, sunny jail.

Having described the board and its responsibilities, how does that affect the shareholder? Obviously, the founders of the company are on this board, with one of them being the managing director. But what about the investors? Wouldn't they want to have a say in these decisions? After all, it's their money at stake as well. Sure they would. And therefore, any group of investors would like to get one or more of its nominees to be a director on the board. Clearly, this would depend on the amount of funding the investors have put in, and is ultimately open to negotiation.

In some cases, usually when the stake of these investors is not very high, they do not get a board seat. Instead, they get what we call 'board observer' status. In other words, one of the investors has the right to be an observer in all board meetings and has access to all information and decisions taken there. And whether it is a board seat or board-observer status, this is documented in the shareholder agreement.

One final comment. As you are aware, the investors will usually own fewer shares in the company than the founders. Potentially, therefore, the founders could get any decision approved by the board or at shareholder meetings. Some of these decisions might not be acceptable to the investors—for instance, if a founder wants to employ a family member in the company or wishes to change the line of business. The SHA provides for such a situation and specifies that the written approval of the investors is required for decisions such as these. And that, by the way, gives us one more legal term—this approval is called 'affirmative assent'.

Equity vs Preference Shares and Liquidation Preference

Aha! You knew it, didn't you? You knew we'd get into high-funda finance. Sure, we need to—you are issuing shares to investors and, believe me, you need to know what you are doing. Now, all along in this book, whenever we have spoken of shares, we have used the term 'equity'. But guess what? You will usually not issue equity shares to your investors. Instead, you will issue preference shares.

Now what are these two animals? First of all, we're sure you've heard of equity shares—these are ordinary shares, such as the ones listed on stock markets. On the other hand, preference shares have more rights than these equity shares. What rights? Well, for starters, any dividend is first paid on preference shares, and only if there is money left after that does the company pay dividend on the equity shares. Of course, you would realize that most early-stage start-ups do not make a profit, let alone pay dividends, so we can safely let this pass. But the other issue is extremely important. What if, god forbid, the company closes down—or, in legal terms, goes into liquidation? We sincerely hope that doesn't happen to you, so let's assume your neighbour's company closes down, although there is still some money left in the bank. What is to be done with this money? This is the interesting part, because the investors who hold preference shares have the first right over this money. In fact, the shareholder agreement can specify how much they get back in case the company goes into liquidation. And this is called 'liquidation preference'. As an example, the SHA could say that the preference shareholders get back 1.5 times what they had originally invested—obviously assuming there is sufficient money available. Only after this is the remainder divided pro rata among the equity shareholders—typically the founders and any other investors.

And now for the 'fun' part. An investor might have invested in your company and is the proud owner of preference shares— with the associated rights. But when a subsequent round is raised, the new investor would definitely want to knock out these rights, wouldn't he? He would want them for himself! And, therefore, all the existing investors might be asked to convert their preference shares into ordinary equity shares, while the new investor gets preference shares—or, at least, gets some additional rights. After all, now he is putting in the money, isn't he? And that's a cycle that gets repeated every time a new investor enters the company. So here's a message to investors: Enjoy your rights as long as you have them!

Right of First Refusal, or ROFR

Aha! Finally, a legal clause that sounds like English. And it means exactly what it says. Let's take an example. You, as the founder, have been able to get funding from a set of early-stage investors, say angels. Later on, a future investor sees an opportunity in your business and wants to buy new shares in the company at an agreed-upon price. For some strange reason, you dislike the original investors and want to bypass them and make an offer to the new investors. However, the angels are smart and they also smell an opportunity. In other words, these angels also want to invest in the company, in place of the new investor. And that, too, on the same terms as those offered to him. Can they do this? Yes, they can. Because the SHA usually has a clause called the 'Right of First Refusal', which gives existing investors the right to buy these shares on the same terms. Only if they pass this offer can the new investor buy these shares. But obviously, the current investors cannot delay their decision indefinitely—and therefore the ROFR clause comes with a pre-defined deadline. The current guys can buy those shares, but after this deadline, they lose this right. Fair, isn't it?

Buy-Back and Drag-Along Rights

The primary objective of investors is to make a profit from their investments, and that, too, within a given time frame (as if you didn't know this). Which basically means that they need to get an exit—hopefully at a significantly higher valuation. Now imagine a situation where several years have passed but there has been no exit for the investors, even though the company has done well. Hopefully this is a rare situation, but it can arise. So what do the investors do? Well, they can request the founders to buy their shares, either personally or get the company to buy them back. If that doesn't happen, the 'Drag Along' clause in the SHA allows investors to find a buyer for their shares. And if the new buyer wants the founders to sell some of their shares, the investors can drag these founders' shares along with their own shares. In other words, the founders are also forced to sell their shares to the new buyer. Fair, isn't it? Incidentally, while the time period for this can vary, it is usually set at seven years.

Tag-Along Rights

Sounds similar to drag-along rights? Actually, it's just the opposite. What if you, as the founder, quietly sell your shares to a buyer, and the buyer does not insist on the original investors exiting? And what if the original investors want to exit? They are now left in the lurch, aren't they? You have sold your shares and gone. And your original investors could be left with shares for which they are not able to get an exit for quite some time. (Of course, you, Mr Founder, are completely ethical and will never do this, but surely there are some founders who will.) You see the problem? So the original investors need an assurance that when the founder sells his shares, he gives them the option of selling their shares as well. Once again on the same terms and conditions. In other words, the original investors have the right to 'tag along' with the founder when he sells his stake. Which is why tag-along rights are also known as 'co-sale' rights.

Just to summarize, the 'buy back and drag along' clause in the agreement ensures that the investors find an eventual exit. And the 'tag along' clause ensures that if the founder exits, he must give the existing investors the right to exit with him.

Finally, you would remember that we had introduced an 'anti-dilution' clause in Chapter 18, when we were discussing valuations. Clearly, that's also part of the SHA.

And that, dear friends, is all we wanted to share about shareholder agreements. Remember, you still need your friendly-neighbourhood lawyer, but at least you now understand what you are getting into.

So happy signing!

Terms of Appointment of the Founders

Let's now go beyond the SHA. Once it has been signed, the investors obviously become part-owners of the company. And the company now issues appointment letters to all the founders. These appointment letters contain several terms and conditions that you must understand.

First of all, there is the concept of vesting of shares. When an investor funds a business, he can ask for the shares of the key founders to be put into an escrow account. To be released over time, based on certain targets or milestones to be met. Which basically means that the founders do not have access to their shares till they have met these targets. For instance, assume that there is one founder in the company and he owns 60 per cent of the shares in the company. The investors may now insist that all these shares are held in an escrow account. At the end of each year, assuming the company meets its targets, 20 per cent of these shares are released to the founder—or, in other words, are vested in the founder. At the end of three years, therefore, all the shares are vested in the founder.

Why would the investors do such a thing? Well, it's a method of putting pressure on the founder to stay on in the company. If he or she leaves before some of their shares are vested, those shares are available to the company and can be given to anyone else—for instance, to other employees as ESOPs.

In the worst case, the investors can even ask for the removal of the founder or founders—with sufficient cause. For instance, if the company performance has been terrible, or worse, if a fraud has been committed. Once again, the shares not vested yet would not be given to him and would be retained within the company, to be given to someone else. And by the way, this is part of the appointment letter of each of the founders.

Of course, if the investors want the founder to be removed without sufficient cause, the founder gets back all his shares—whether or not they have been vested. And that's only fair, isn't it?

And then there are two more clauses that are invariably part of the terms of appointment. Clauses that we call 'non-compete' and 'non-solicitation'. What's 'non-compete'? Fairly straightforward: In case the founder quits the company, he cannot compete with it for a given period—usually five years. And 'non-solicitation' means that he cannot take away an existing client.

What Happens in Practice

And now for some hush-hush advice. Strictly between you and us—please do not disclose it to anyone else. We've given you lots of legal terms that you'll find in the SHA as well as in the term sheet. First of all, most of these terms are open to negotiation between the founder and the investors. And secondly, they are often not enforced. It actually depends on the stage the start-up is in. So if it's an early-stage start-up, where each angel has put in just Rs 5 lakh each, no one wants to go to court to fight a battle. And, therefore, these clauses are used more to pressurize the founders. However, at later stages, when the funding goes into several millions of dollars, the stakes are high. That is where both founders and investors follow the agreement more strictly.

Either way, there is one thing you must remember as a founder. If you violate a clause, the investors may not take you to court—but that's not the point. Investors are a small group. And word spreads like wildfire. More than court battles, it's your reputation that matters. After all, for your next round of funding—or even for your next start-up—you don't want investors to say, 'Ah, this is the guy—no way we're going to fund him', do you?

The Impact of the Coronavirus—or Any Other Crisis

Dear reader, this part is critical. For starters, let's look at term sheets. Remember, a term sheet is something like an MoU. And, therefore, it is *non-binding*. It simply says, 'In case we finally go ahead, these are the broad terms and conditions we have agreed to.' Therefore, even in the best of times, investors might not invest, in spite of having signed a term sheet. And in bad times—such as during the COVID-19 crisis or the global financial crisis of 2008, well, they have every reason to back out. So a term sheet is one step in the process, but it does not guarantee that the funds will finally come in.

And what about the SHA? Now this is a legal document, and is therefore binding. However, all shareholder agreements have something called a 'force majeure' clause. Which simply means that if there is a significant event that is neither anticipated nor controllable, some of the clauses in the SHA can become void. Effectively they would not be valid any more. And that's a sobering thought, isn't it?

So that ends our spiel on legal terms that you are likely to encounter. We hope you've understood them, because you'll have to sign on them. One last point. We thought of putting in one complete SHA in the appendix, so that you are aware of what you are likely to sign. But typical SHAs are perhaps forty pages long, and that would have made this book unaffordable for struggling founders. So we haven't included the SHA. But we have included a draft term sheet, which is a lot smaller. And that will give you a feel of the SHA that you will ultimately sign. But please, please ignore the long, complex and sometimes unending sentences in the document. You must realize that lawyers need to survive and thrive. If they were to create simple documents that you and I can understand, why would we go to them in the first place? Agreed? So any such legal document is invariably written in such a way that, on reading it, the first thing you would do is reach out to your friendly-neighbourhood lawyer. Which is fine—in any case, you need a lawyer before you sign it. So just go to your lawyer, and you'll be okay!

Let's Meet Rajul Garg, Founder and Managing Partner, Leo Capital India Advisors

So, ladies and gentlemen, you've met some of the biggest and most successful entrepreneurs in the digital world. And got solid advice on running your business as well as raising funds from all of them. It's now time to meet a VC, Rajul Garg, the founder and managing partner of Leo Capital Advisors. An IIT Delhi alumnus, this is what Rajul had to say:

> You need to understand how VCs operate. They float funds that investors invest in. And then they use the money raised to invest in start-ups—but typically beyond the angel level. Since the purpose of the fund is to give returns to their investors, we need to understand the psychology of the investor. Remember, investors have the option of the stock market, where they have lower risk as well as high liquidity. Start-up investments carry higher risk, and, at the same time, these investments are illiquid—you cannot exit till you find another investor who is willing to enter. And, therefore, investors in a typical VC fund

expect significantly higher returns than they would in the stock market—typically 25 per cent or even higher in many cases. And, therefore, this is the kind of target returns the VC aims at.

It is also known that only a few out of the investments the fund has made will click and give bumper returns. Therefore, each investment must have huge potential, so that even if one of them works out, it makes up for all the other duds. And, therefore, the first thing all of us VCs look for is the size of the market. Unless this is extremely large, we cannot get the bumper growth that our investors expect.

Of course, the team of founders is critical—if we don't get the right guys here, how will they take advantage of the huge potential? Clarity of thought, the presence of a strong vision as well as a detailed plan, and the execution ability to take the company there is critical. What's the proof of all this? Simple. We look at what they've done so far—the traction, the moat they have built, etc.

One final word of advice to young entrepreneurs. Don't bluff—you'll be caught in no time. And no investor likes a founder who bluffs his way through. We all want honest, genuine investors. And don't drop names—you may have been to other VCs, but don't try to impress me, or anyone else for that matter, by dropping these names. Focus on your business, and hopefully we'll have a deal.

That was great advice, Rajul. Thanks a lot.

Incidentally, you guys would have noticed that most experienced people have given you similar advice—whether it is entrepreneurs, angel investors or VCs. Which is natural, isn't it? After all, there are just a few simple guidelines to follow to build a successful business. So follow this advice, and all the best!

21

So What Should You Do?

At long last we come to the end of this book. You've read stories about successes, and you've also read stories about failures. You've met founders who are just about starting up, and you've also met founders who have really made it big. You've seen how businesses are grown and managed, and how you can get funding. By now you probably have advice pouring out of your ears. But remember, all this is simply advice. What you do with it is entirely up to you.

So what do you do? Well, first of all, we hope you've actually read the book, and haven't skipped to this page. If you haven't read it, please do so now.

Next, we would strongly recommend that you evaluate your start-up—or potential start-up—using our PERSISTENT framework. As we've been saying all along, successful start-ups tend to fit into this framework, whereas failures miss out on one or more parameters. And you want to be successful, don't you? Importantly, this framework is not only meant for investors to evaluate your business—even more than that, it's meant for you. Of course, you must bear in mind that it's a set of guidelines and not a formula. It cannot guarantee success—for that matter, even God cannot—but it can certainly improve your chances of doing well.

We then come to the subject of funding. Please, please do not look for funding simply because it's fashionable to do so and you can quietly drop valuations at parties. Get funding if you need it. And if you do need it, start with your family and friends. These are people who will not ask too many questions and will not impose conditions either. Of course, once you've exhausted that source (or exhausted your family), go to angels and later to VCs. But don't worry too much about the valuation at which you get the money—if you need it, you need it. Just get it and it'll help you grow your business.

More than just the money, it's important to get it from the right investor. Someone whose thinking is aligned with yours and who is ideally passionate about the business as well. Someone who can add value and not keep breathing down your neck asking for a quick exit.

Of course, you've got to make a business plan, which you will pitch to potential investors. While doing so, remember your WYKM—'What's Your Key Message?'. But please, please do not try to fool the investors. Do not use financial jugglery. Believe it or not, investors are very savvy people with loads of experience and they'll see through it. And that'll be the end of your funding dreams.

We do hope you make it to the next step, where the investors give you a term sheet. And finally, of course, the real thing, where you negotiate and sign the shareholder agreement, and get all those yummy cheques! Most importantly, please involve your lawyer at both these stages—your investors will bring in all their legal firepower, and you are definitely not an expert on the subject (unless, of course, you are a lawyer yourself). And once that is signed, just sit back, relax and enjoy the money flowing in . . .

Well, that's not really correct. When running a start-up, you cannot really sit back and relax. As you've heard from many of the founders in this book, it's a lifetime's commitment. It demands hard work. And patience. And more patience. And still more. But at the end of it all, it's more than worth it.

Dear founder, we'd love to see you succeed. And we do hope that somewhere, somehow, this book has a teeny-weeny role to play in your success. Either way, do get back to us and share your feedback. Our email ids are dhruvn55@gmail.com and sushanto@leadangels.in. We'd be delighted to hear from you. And, who knows—you might end up with a lead role in our next book!

So from both of us to you: All the best, and happy starting up.

Appendix

A Draft Term Sheet

For Investment in ABC Services Private Limited

Date: 20 December 2019

The intent of this document is to describe, for negotiation purposes only, the principal terms of the proposed investment by [•] ("**Investor(s)**") in ABC SERVICES PRIVATE LIMITED ("**Company**"). The obligations of the Investors outlined in this document are subject to satisfactory completion of due diligence, internal approvals of the Investor and execution of appropriate definitive agreements (the "**Definitive Agreements**").

If this term sheet remains unsigned until [*date*], the Investor(s) at its option may immediately terminate discussions with the Promoters/Company or change any or all pricing, terms and conditions contained herein.

Investor(s) agree to make an investment in ABC SERVICES PRIVATE LIMITED on the terms and conditions detailed below.

A.	**Issuer**	ABC SERVICES PRIVATE LIMITED ("Company")
B.	**Definitions & General Provisions**	
1.	Promoters	
2.	Investors	(a) [•] (Investor Name and Investment Amount) (b) [•] (c) [•] The Investors hereinabove shall have rights in their individual capacity as well as a group. Any decision pertaining to rights associated with the group, such as the issue of company being acquired, nomination of board member, etc., shall be taken by a simple majority vote of the Investors and all Investors shall abide by the majority decision.
3.	Proposed Transaction	Aggregate investment of Rs _____lakh subject to a maximum of Rs _____lakh at the option of the investors.
4.	Valuation	The investment is based on a pre-money valuation of Rs _____ lakh The post-money valuation of the Company shall be: i. Amount invested at first closing plus Rs _____ lakh ii. Post-money valuation in first closing plus amount invested in second closing.

5.	Staged Investment	The investment shall be staged as follows: (a) First Tranche: A minimum of Rs ____lakh on first closing, subject to a maximum of Rs ____lakh at the option of the investor on first closing. (b) Second Tranche: A minimum of Rs ____ lakh on first closing, subject to a maximum of Rs ____ lakh at the option of the investor on second closing.
6.	Use of Proceeds	The Investor(s) and the Company agree that the First Tranche will be utilized by the Company for the Agreed Business Plan.
7.	Securities to be Issued	[•] Preference Shares at a share price of Rs [•] per share (including any share premium) as set out in Clause 10.
8.	Terms of Investor Shares	• Dividend rate: The same as is declared for the equity shareholders and calculated on an as converted basis. • Priority in Payment: Pari-passu with other series of preference shares when issued and senior to common shares.
9.	Current Shareholding Pattern	<table><tr><td>**Name**</td><td>**No. of Shares**</td><td>**Ownership [%]**</td></tr><tr><td></td><td></td><td></td></tr><tr><td></td><td></td><td></td></tr><tr><td></td><td></td><td></td></tr><tr><td>Total</td><td></td><td>100%</td></tr></table>

10.	Post Investment Capitalization Table (Fully Diluted)	Immediately following completion of the Proposed Transaction at a total investment of Rs _____ lakh, the share capital of the Company shall be constituted as set out below: In case the investment is less, the same shall be on pro-rata basis.

Name	No. of Shares	Ownership [%]
ESOP		10%

Name	No. of Shares	Ownership [%]

11.	ESOP	The stock option pool will be created, before the completion of this investment so as to comprise 10% of the company's total share capital on a Fully Diluted Basis.
12.	Expected Date of Closing	*First Closing*: 28 February 2020 *Second Closing:* As mentioned in Clause 18 herein.
13.	Promoters' and Senior Management Team Commitment	(a) The Promoters and senior management team will enter into employment agreements with the Company prior to execution of the Definitive Agreements. The agreements will include standard clauses like non-compete, non-solicitation, and confidential information to the satisfaction of the Investor.

	(b) Promoters and the Company have developed and/or own certain technologies, inventions and other intellectual property (collectively, **"Intellectual Property"**). Promoters agree that they shall legally protect and assign all such Intellectual Property to the Company before the closing of this investment. (c) Promoters agree not to sell, transfer or encumber their shares in the Company for a period of 3 years from the date of this investment ("Lock-in Period").
14. Liquidation Preference	In case of a Liquidation Event, the preference shares will, at the option of the Investor be converted to equity shares, and the Investor will then be entitled to receive whichever of the following is higher: (a) an amount equal to 2 times their investment, OR (b) their pro-rata share of the proceeds Except for a Qualified IPO or a Strategic Sale, a sale, merger or consolidation of the Company in which its shareholders do not retain a majority of the voting power in the surviving company, or a sale of all or substantially all the Company's assets or liquidation, dissolution or winding up of the Company, would each be deemed to be a **"Liquidation Event"**. **"Qualified IPO"** means closing of an underwritten public offering of equity shares of the Company, whereby the equity shares of the Company are listed and admitted for trading on any stock exchange at a final price which offers the Investors the Minimum Valuation as defined in clause 16(b) below.

	"Strategic Sale" means sale of majority shareholding (>50%) of the Company for cash or listed securities as approved by the Investor. Such sale offers the Investor, the Minimum Valuation as defined in clause 16(b) below. Nothing contained in this clause shall apply to a sale or transfer of the shares or assets of the Company if the Investors have provided their prior written consent to such sale or transfer.
15. Anti-Dilution	Full weighted broad-based average dilution protection in the event of any further issuance of shares at a price per share lower than the purchase price paid by the Investors. Proportional adjustment in the event of bonus, share splits, equity dividend, reclassifications and the like.
16. Exit	IPO or a Strategic Sale: At any time after March 2025, the Investor may require the Company to make a Qualified IPO or a Strategic Sale, provided a Qualified IPO or a Strategic Sale can be executed if the Company has achieved revenue of Rs 75 crores. In such an event, the Company and the Promoters shall do all acts necessary to execute the IPO or the Strategic Sale successfully. (a) Buy Back: In the event the Company has not completed a Qualified IPO or a Strategic Sale, by March 2025, the Investor at its option may require the Company to provide the exit to the Investor by way of buy back at the higher of: i. Fair Market Value (as per independent valuation by Investment Banker(s) of international repute), OR

<table>
<tr>
<td></td>
<td>

ii.   The return of the investment with an IRR of 25% from the date of investment till the date of exit ("**Exit**")

(such amount shall hereinafter be referred to as "**Minimum Valuation**")

In the event that the Company is unable to buy back the Investor's stake, the Promoters shall make best efforts to find a buyer for the Investors' stake in the Company to provide Exit to the Investors.

(b) Tag Along Right: If any Promoter wishes to transfer any of his shares in the Company, the Investors shall have the right to include in such transfer a proportional number of the Investor Shares (on an as converted basis) on the same terms and conditions as applicable to the sale of such Promoter shares. If, however, the proposed transfer would result in the aggregate shareholding of the Promoters falling below 26% of the share capital of the Company, Investors shall be entitled to sell all of the Investor Shares (on an as converted basis) as part of such transfer.

(c) Drag Along Rights of Investors: In case the Company or the Promoters fail to provide the exit options provided above or a buy-back option as contemplated above by March 2025, the Investors will have the right to sell, merge or liquidate the Company at their own option at the prevailing fair market value. In such an event, the Promoters shall ensure that all the other common shareholders, preferred shareholders, management team and

</td>
</tr>
</table>

		employees, shall be obliged to offer their shares in full, along with the Promoters, to facilitate exit to the Investor. If the Company raises new funds / investment before 2020 to provide the Investors exit with the Minimum Valuation, the drag along rights under this clause may be waived by the Investors, subject to such terms and conditions as the Investors may deem fit in their sole discretion. This drag-along right shall terminate on the happening of the IPO, a Strategic Sale or a Buy-Back by the Company where the Investors realize their Minimum Valuation. For further financing, the promoters shall make best efforts to negotiate retention of this clause. If however, the potential investors do not agree, then on a request by the promoters, the Investors shall consider postponement or waiver of this clause, without undue delay.
17.	Conditions Precedent to First Closing	The proposed investment is subject to:
		(a) Due Diligence: Completion of due diligence on the business plan of the Company. The Investors will have the right to appoint auditors and advisers to conduct financial and legal due diligence of the Company, the scope of which may be decided by the Investors in their own discretion. The Company shall bear all costs incurred in connection with due diligence review.
		(b) Approvals: Receipt of all regulatory and statutory approvals and approval of the Board/Management Committee of the Investors for investment in the Company.

	(c) Documentation: Completion of Definitive Agreements and all other required documentation to the mutual satisfaction of both Parties including the due diligence exercise. The cost of documentation of the agreements will be borne by the Company. No material or adverse changes in the information submitted by the Company.
18. Conditions Precedent to Second Closing	
19. Conversion Rate	The Conversion Rate for the Preference Shares would be based on the post-money valuation described above. Conversion Rate would be suitably adjusted for any new issue of shares or share equivalents, stock splits, stock dividends, etc. The Investors may exercise their option to convert the Investor Shares, at their sole discretion, up to a Qualified IPO or Strategic Sale.
20. Automatic Conversion	The Investor Shares shall automatically be converted into Equity Shares, at the Purchase Price, upon a Qualified IPO or Strategic Sale.
21. Pre-emptive Right and Right of First Offer	The Investors will have a right of first offer to: (a) subscribe up to its pro rata share on a Fully Diluted Basis of any equity securities offered by the Company other than in any IPO event, on the same price and terms and conditions as the Company offers such securities to other potential investors.

		(b) purchase up to all of the shares proposed to be sold and transferred by any of the Promoters of the Company. These rights would terminate upon the closing of a Qualified IPO or a Strategic Sale. Notwithstanding the foregoing, shares held by any of the Promoters / management team members, shall be subject to the lock-in restriction to the extent required by the applicable law or the regulator.
22.	Voting Rights, Protective Provisions and Other Rights	The Company agrees that the following actions will be done only with the prior approval of the Investors/Investor Director: • Merger, acquisition, increase or decrease in authorized capital or, new investments or any other form of capital restructuring, excluding this round of Investment. • Dividend payments and buyback of shares. • Sale or transfer of any intellectual property/ intangible asset, which is material to the operations of the Company. • Sale or transfer of a significant part of the business of the Company. • Any changes in Memorandum of Association and Articles of Association. • Any change of statutory auditor. • The pricing and timing and all other terms and conditions of an IPO or an offer for sale of shares. • The acquisition of any other business, diversification or expansion. • Any major changes in the Company's financial year or in its accounting policies.

- Any decision to hire/fire senior management employees, identified in the Definitive Agreements, or any change in their terms of employment.
- The extension of loans to any party except employees.
- Any related party transactions of value more than Rs 50,000.
- Any material changes in the Company's business plan, including entering any new lines of business and incorporation or winding down of any subsidiary.
- Raising new loans (except working capital loans) not in the course of ordinary business, involving amounts exceeding Rs 5,00,000.
- Raising working capital loans involving amounts exceeding Rs 5,00,000.
- Any incurrence by the Company of absolute or contingent indebtedness for borrowed money and the terms of such borrowing, which are outside the purview of the approved business plan of the Company.

Notwithstanding the above, the Investor will have the right to vote on all the matters requiring shareholders' approval on an as-converted basis. The consent rights of the Investors shall terminate on the happening of the Qualified IPO, a Strategic Sale or a Buy-Back by the Company or if the cumulative shareholding of the Investors in the Company falls below 5% by reason of sale by any of the Investors of their shares in the Company or where the Investors realize their minimum valuation. It is hereby clarified that a decrease in Investor shareholding due to any reason other than voluntary sale of shares shall not affect the consent rights of the Investors, in any manner.

23. Board Seat	The Investor shall have a right to nominate at least one Director on the Board of the Company. The presence of Investor Director/s will be required for purposes of the quorum for any board meeting of the Company. The Investor Director/s shall also have the option to attend the board meetings through video conferencing.
24. Other Covenants	• The Company shall modify its Memorandum and Articles of Association in consultation with and to the satisfaction of the Investors to reflect the Definitive Agreements. • The Investors shall receive standard information rights including audited annual financial reports, unaudited quarterly financial reports, annual budget and business plan, board packages, as well as standard audit/inspection rights. • Standard financial reports shall be sent to the Investors/Investors' representative on the board on a monthly basis.
25. Representations and Warranties	The Definitive Agreements will have customary representations and warranties of the Company and the Promoters with appropriate indemnification for the Investor.
26. Confidentiality	The Company agrees to keep the contents of this term sheet confidential. Neither party shall make any public disclosure of this term sheet without mutual consent.
27. Exclusivity	The Company and the Promoters will work exclusively with the Investor for sixty (60) days from the date of signing this document, shall not, directly or indirectly, solicit, have discussions or provide any information to any other potential investor, without written approval from the Investor during this period. The Company shall not issue shares of any class to any party until Closing.

Investors   **Promoters**

_____   _____
[*Name*]

                               _____

Company

_____   _____

ABC Services Private Limited
Title:
Company Stamp:

Acknowledgements

When we finished writing this book, we sat down to write this section. And we realized with a start that it wasn't really our book!

Yes, it does have our names on the cover. And, of course, all the jokes are strictly ours. But it would be unfair to call it our book. Simply because there have been many, many people who have contributed in a huge way to making it possible.

Here are some of them . . .

First of all, Sanjeev Bikhchandani, the founder and vice chairman of Naukri.com, and one of the first to bring start-up culture to the country. Sanjeev was kind enough to share with us the phenomenal experiences he has been through in his entrepreneurial journey. And when we requested him to write the foreword for this book, he readily agreed.

Some of the major founders and investors in the world of start-ups—Deep Kalra of MakeMyTrip, Pradeep Gupta of CyberMedia, Dinesh Agarwal of IndiaMART, Yashish Dahiya of PolicyBazaar and PaisaBazaar, Sairee Chahal of SHEROES and Rajul Garg of Leo Capital. All of these people took out time from their ever-so-busy schedules and shared their views with us—which made this book far more powerful than it would otherwise have been.

Our young friends, including the founders of the companies we have invested in—Nakul Kumar of Cashify, Samant Sikka of SQRRL, Jaineel Aga of Planet Superheroes, Abhishek Barari of MyCuteOffice, Chaitanya Jha and Abhinav Imandi of QACCO, Amit Grover of AHA Taxis, Aman Garg of Greymeter and Tushar Agarwal of Uno Finance. It was fascinating going through this journey together with them. We must also say that, hardened and grizzled veterans of the start-up industry we might be, but we have learnt so, so, so much from these youngsters. And, of course, those founders that we learnt from but whose names have not been mentioned in the book. Thanks a lot, guys—we still remember you.

Many, many colleagues and ex-colleagues at Lead Angels have contributed to our fascinating journey through the world of start-ups. And have put up with two 'slightly cracked' old men—although we believe we are still young. We wish we could name all of them, but that would mean a few more pages (and we're reasonably certain you would refuse to bear that cost). So a truncated list would be: Manish Johari, Suman Sengupta, Ishan Jindal, Bipin Shah, Sera Arora, Rajiv Ranka, Monaaz Mistry and Chiranjeev Anand.

Penguin Random House India has been a great publisher, starting with our editors Radhika Marwah and Ujjaini Dasgupta. Believe it or not, Radhika was in touch with us right through her marriage, which was scheduled bang in the middle of the publication of this book. And all of you know how demanding an Indian marriage can be. Radhika was the one person who insisted that we bring humour into a serious subject like funding—and for that alone we are eternally grateful to her. Along with all of her colleagues who worked brilliantly behind the scenes to get this book to the shape it finally took.

These were the thanks from both the authors—Dhruv and Sushanto. And now for specific thanks from each of us.

From Dhruv: First and foremost my wife Rajni, who has wholeheartedly supported an eccentric husband—who suddenly decided to renounce the world (temporarily, of course) and write this book full-time. Rajni and my daughter, Malvika—who, by the way, is into the world of finance—have been my silent editors, going through page after page of this book. Incidentally, left to myself, this book might have become a pure humorous book, with just a wee bit about funding. But because I occasionally listened to their advice, it remains a book about funding—with humour in the background. And my son Siddharth, a lawyer, has been my sounding board for all the legal issues that you will find towards the end of the book.

Finally, of course, how can I forget my parents? They have encouraged me in whatever I have ever wanted to do, ever since I was born. Or, more accurately, from the time I was two years old and knew what the hell was going on.

From Sushanto: I would like to thank my wife, Ranjana Roy, who supported me through this project. Among many, many other things, she allowed the lights to be on at night for me to write my part. And, of course, my late father, who encouraged me to follow my creative instincts. It didn't get me the desired marks in my school essays, but after all these years it has culminated in this book.

And from both of us: By the way, we have given you all these names so any blame can be laid in the right quarters . . .